Once Upon a Line...

Inspector Ron Russell heads down Ryde Pier after examining the progress with reconstruction works.

Tim Genower

Previous page: No. 16 *Ventnor* approaches Ryde Pier Head with a train from Ventnor on 7th August 1965. Note the other O2 class 0-4-4 tank waiting on the 'down' line, just beyond the scissor cross-over points, left.

Tony Scarsbrook

Once Upon a Line...

Volume 4

Andrew Britton

Oxford Publishing Co.

First published in 1994.

A catalogue record for this book is available from the British Library.

ISBN 0 86093 513 2

Oxford Publishing Co. is an imprint of Haynes Publishing, Sparkford, near Yeovil, Somerset BA22 7JJ

Printed Great Britain by Butler & Tanner Ltd, Frome and London

Typeset in Times Roman Medium by MS Filmsetting Limited, Frome, Somerset

Dedication

This volume is dedicated to the following special people who helped me produce these books: my wife Annette, Dad and Mum, Dick Blenkinsop, Ken West, Jimmy James, Owen Attrill, Nelson Parsons, Richard Newman, Patrick Kingston, Ian Wightmore, Mike 'Chuff' Downer, Tim Cooper, the late Eddie Spears, Barry Poultney, Peter Nicholson of OPC, and that motivator of steam enthusiasts – particularly the Isle of Wight variety, wildlife artist David Shepherd OBE. None of this would have been possible without your continued love and help. God bless you all.

Acknowledgements

The success of the *Once Upon a Line...* series can be attributed to all the magnificent help received. Not one person has ever turned me away when contacted for a request for assistance. Dick Blenkinsop has been particularly generous with his time and help with all matters relating to the photographic content of this book. Barry Poultney and Barry Walker Photography of Leamington Spa have quite often burned the midnight oils to achieve my impossible requests. Once again I am delighted that the Island railway cartoonist, Jimmy James, has come out of retirement to produce some excellent work just for Volume Four.

On a day to day basis much encouragement has been offered to see this project to its conclusion by Richard Newman, Dick Blenkinsop, my wife Annette and the children – Jonathan, Mark and Matthew, plus my parents. I am also sincerely honoured that Patrick Kingston has taken valuable time off from his royal trains to write the Foreword to this book. This is greatly appreciated.

Considerable assistance has been given by the Isle of Wight Steam Railway, who once again launched the last book in a similar fashion to Volumes One and Two, by hosting a grand reunion of railway staff. At Haven Street station, the contributors to the *Once Upon a Line...* books were given VIP treatment which included a steam-hauled ride behind 'Terrier' tank No. 11 *Newport* bearing the OPC headboard. This was a day to remember, as hopefully will be the launch of Volume Four. All this was due entirely to those kind volunteers at Haven Street.

Contents

On the left No. 22 *Brading* waits to depart from Ryde Pier Head with a train to Shanklin and Ventnor, while No. 20 *Shanklin* prepares to depart with a train for Newport and Cowes.

J. R. G. Griffiths

Foreword
by Patrick Kingston

A brief mention to a fellow railway enthusiast that I had been asked to write a foreword for Volume Four of *Once Upon a Line*... brought the comment, "surely there can't be enough unpublished material for yet another book on the Isle of Wight railways." Suprisingly there is!

Andrew Britton's name is synonymous with railways on the Isle of Wight, sadly now but a shadow of a once extensive system. It is only recently that I discovered Andrew isn't a native of the Island, being born in the Warwickshire town of Leamington Spa. However, it was his father, born just across the Solent at Southampton, who encouraged Andrew's boyhood fascination with railways and in particular the Island's railways in their twilight years. The fact that much of the system was closed during his formative years gave him, on achieving maturity, the incentive to collect all kinds of material, to share with others; the joy of watching those little tank hauled passenger trains that were so much a part of a much loved transport facility.

Volume One was published in 1983, by which time Andrew Britton was already planning a second volume, to be closely followed by a third. Andrew's enthusiasm and meticulous research justifies Volume Four which he confirms will be the last. Who knows!

Queen Victoria's home, Osborne House, brought Royal patronage to the Island's railways. Indeed, the Queen herself expressed a wish for a private station at Whippingham on the Newport–Ryde line. Unusually, Queen Victoria noted in her Journal for Saturday 11th February 1888 that she had made her first journey on an Isle of Wight train for a visit to the Royal National Hospital for Consumption at Ventnor. This reference indicates Her Majesty was well pleased with the Island's railways. Volume Two contains a reference to a subsequent little known Royal journey, by the Queen, then Princess Elizabeth, and her sister Princess Margaret, who as young girls were passengers on an ordinary service train from Cowes to Newport, prior to World War II.

In the more environmentally conscious 1990s, it is quite probable more of the Island's railways could have survived. Memories of former days live on through preservation of the Isle of Wight Steam Railway between Haven Street and Smallbrook Junction. Volume Four, as in previous volumes, provides the opportunity for the reader to rediscover the closed lines, but also the vital ingredient of what made them tick – the staff. It is the experiences of railwaymen and women of all grades, past and present, whose contributions to Andrew's *Once Upon a Line*... books provide the personal flavour of life as employees in a place many people refer to affectionately as 'The Island.'

My association with the Isle of Wight railways has been as a holidaymaker, whose curiosity to go there was fired by the romantic title boards that were once carried by the Southern's electric expresses from London, proclaiming, 'Waterloo–Portsmouth and the Isle of Wight'. I feel privileged to be associated with Andrew's concluding Volume and have little doubt that the four *Once Upon a Line*... books will be sought after, in future years, not only by railway lovers, but those wishing to discover the pulse of life in earlier, more genteel years.

Patrick Kingston

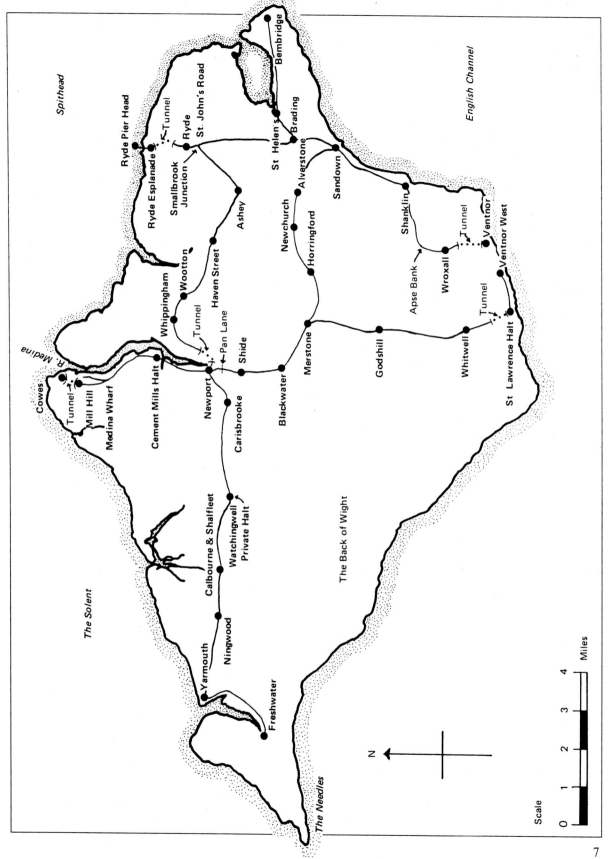

Spithead

English Channel

Ryde Pier Head
Ryde Esplanade
Tunnel
Ryde
St. John's Road
Smallbrook Junction
Bembridge
St Helen's
Brading
Alverstone
Sandown
Newchurch
Horringford
Ashey
Wootton
Whippingham
Haven Street
Tunnel
Pan Lane
Shide
Shanklin
Apse Bank
Ventnor
Tunnel
Wroxall
Ventnor West
Merstone
Godshill
Whitwell
Tunnel
St Lawrence Halt
Blackwater
Cement Mills Halt
Newport
Carisbrooke
R. Medina
Cowes
Tunnel
Mill Hill
Medina Wharf

The Solent

Calbourne & Shalfleet
Watchingwell Private Halt
Ningwood
Yarmouth
Freshwater

The Back of Wight

The Needles

N

Scale
0   1   2   3   4
Miles

7

Preface

'All good things come to an end', so the saying goes and this really is the end of the line for the *Once Upon a Line...* series. What started out as a chance remark by former Smallbrook Junction signalman, Eddie Spears back in April 1979, has ended up in the publication of four volumes, several reunions of railway staff and countless hours of fun.

During my researches, I have collected many hours, if not weeks of taped interviews. Much of the information contained on these tapes has been transcribed for publication. However, I have used editorial discretion and omitted much controversial material, particularly relating to the latter day closures of the Island lines. As a history teacher, I realise that it is essential to find evidence to support new discoveries contained in the text. This has been done either by tracing photographs or by verifying stories with other railway staff. My test has always been, "Would it stand up in a court of law?" The answer has always been, "Yes!".

The appeal of all four of these volumes to the general railway enthusiast is that it is possible to dip into the books at will. Some readers have written to me to relate that the books have been read as regular 'bed time books' or, as 'holiday read'. From the academics, the *Once Upon a Line...* series is now recognised as a social, as well as a railway history. However, I take most satisfaction from the comments of the families of railway staff who cherish the recorded memories of loved ones and see their reminiscences preserved in print for future generations.

The first three volumes have proved to be a tremendous success and have sold world wide, as far afield as Australia, South Africa, Canada and the United States. I was amazed to hear that scientific workers at the South Pole Research Station had circulated copies amongst themselves, during off duty hours! The extraordinary appeal of the railways of the Isle of Wight could be justifiably said to have attracted a world-wide interest.

I hope in some small way that these books have focused interest on the preserved remnants of the Island railway network. Since 1979, the Isle of Wight Steam Railway has progressed a long way from the short two-mile line twixt Wootton and Haven Street, to a professional five-mile operation linking up with British Rail Network SouthEast at Smallbrook Junction. What sets this magnificent railway apart from other preserved lines is that it is operated with a unique collection of original Isle of Wight locomotives and rolling stock. If after reading this book you have enjoyed it, then head for the Isle of Wight Steam Railway and relive those days of glory at first hand.

Chapter One – The Ryde Pier Head–Ventnor Line

Ron Russell

I was the last Island Area Inspector during the steam era and commenced my duties on the Island in 1960. My duties included overseeing all traffic operation embracing signalmen, guards and station staff. I worked a basic 3.30am till 4.30pm working day, but I was on continuous 24-hour a day call, being the only Area Inspector. This was a bit of a bind as it was possible to be called out at 3.30am when problems arose with the first trains of the day – the Cowes and Ventnor mail trains. Generally I would be called out to all derailments, signalling irregularities, accidents to staff and similar day to day railway problems, such as flooding in Ventnor and Ryde tunnels.

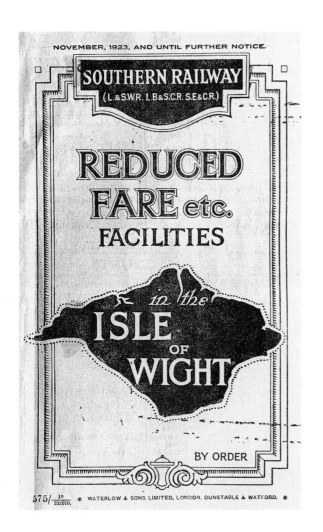

NOVEMBER, 1923, AND UNTIL FURTHER NOTICE.

SOUTHERN RAILWAY
(L.&S.W.R. L.B.&S.C.R. S.E.&C.R.)

REDUCED FARE etc. FACILITIES

in the

ISLE OF WIGHT

BY ORDER

575/- ¹⁰⁄₂₃₂₀₁₀   ✳ WATERLOW & SONS LIMITED, LONDON, DUNSTABLE & WATFORD. ✳

Call outs to railway accidents on the Island was not a glamorous affair. I recall attending the unpleasant incident near my home at Brading, when O2 tank No. 14 *Fishbourne* hit a herd of full grown steers weighing about 15 cwt each, which were sheltering from the cold under Truckells Bridge. About six or seven beasts were killed and the engine had the leading steps knocked off and the side rod was bent, as described by Driver Ginger Minter in *Once Upon a Line... Volume One*. It was my job to supervise restoration of the service and clean up the mess. This was a horrible task as the only way to remove the dead carcasses of the cows was to attach them one by one to the draw bar of an O2 tank and literally drag them along the line to Brading station where they could be removed.

The other memorable railway accident that I had to attend on the Island was likewise described in *Volume One* by Driver Nelson Parsons. This involved the derailment of the 5.08pm train from Newport, which was being propelled from the sidings by O2 tank No. 14 *Fishbourne*. This was a messy job to clear up with carriage stock and locomotive derailed. As Nelson described, a signal post was demolished and even the signal box steps were destroyed! The big problem which I encountered was that so much of the track and wooden sleepers were torn up.

One unexpected call out was to supervise the clearance of snow which fell on Christmas Day night in 1962. I knew nothing about the blizzard until Signalman Roy Way knocked the door of my house on Boxing Day morning. "Look at this, Ron. The roads are blocked between Ryde and Ventnor, and Ryde and Cowes", pointed out a chilled Signalman Way. When I got dressed I struggled through the deep snow outside my Station House at Brading and looked in almost disbelief at the depth of snow between the platforms in Brading station – they were covered and the lines were buried at platform height. I sent for all the permanent way staff I could get my hands on to assist with clearing the snow. Some accompanied the Ryde-Ventnor mail train hauled by engine No. 29 *Alverstone*. That train left Ryde at 8.15am and didn't arrive at Ventnor until 7.30pm. I gathered from the driver of No. 29, Jim Hunnybun, that they got stuck at Rowborough Bridge, Brading and Sandown stations and on Apse Bank. The other mail train to Newport and Cowes left Ryde shortly after 8.45am and this time I made sure that there was an engine at both ends of the train. I believe we had No. 21 *Sandown* at the front end and No. 24 *Calbourne* at the rear. We made slow progress from Smallbrook Junction and halted frequently to shovel the snow clear. Heading out of Newport I was on the footplate of the leading engine, No. 21. The driver spotted a figure walking through the snow towards us and he flagged us down. He warned us to take great care at milepost 12 as there were deep snow drifts. Well, we could not see this milepost as it was buried, but we did feel the whole O2 tank locomotive rise just like a hovercraft! How we managed to remain on the rails I will never know, but we did make it through to Cowes eventually. Everyone was wet and cold but they had done a wonderful job.

One of my many duties was to 'pass-out' and examine new signalmen on the Island. The first signalman I was given to examine was Bill Moore at Brading signal box. The convention for passing out new signalmen is that the tutor-signalman should leave the box when the inspector attends to examine the candidate. On this occasion Signalman Roy Way and I were chatting away for about half an hour in the box, from nine until half past nine

one morning, whilst the candidate, Bill Moore, operated the box. Signalman Way enquired if he could go, to avoid any embarrassment during the examination. However, just before he set off down the steps he admitted that he had hoped to be free at this time as he had arranged to assist the undertaker at a funeral in the local Roman Catholic church! One can only wonder what would have been the outcome at the burial if I had not released him from duty.

An average day of duty for me would generally comprise the following pattern. I would commence work at Newport station in the offices, where I would spend from 8.30am till 9.15am sorting through the paper work. Perhaps we would then have a short hierarchy meeting to discuss any problems or points of interest, before I set off around the Island lines visiting signal boxes and stations. Any engineering works at weekends or during the night would sometimes require my presence to ensure smooth running etc. Likewise, I would sort out any single-line working rosters or token failures. An interesting duty was to supervise pigeon-race releases from the Island – something that has long since gone. In the last few years of

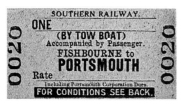

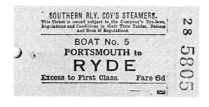

PILE DRIVING ON RYDE PIER – THE OLD WAY

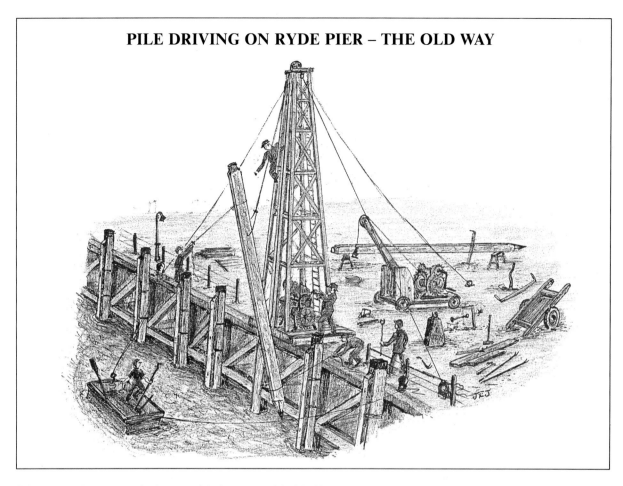

This was a continuous operation because of the large area of the Pier Head; and up to 1960 no machinery other than a manual winch was ever used to lift the 60ft long 14in × 14in greenheart piles. they were prepared at the Pier Head by experienced timbermen, conveyed to site, and transferred to the 50ft high wooden frame by manpower alone.

steam railway enthusiasts caused a few headaches for me with trespassing on railway property – particularly at Smallbrook Junction, climbing up railway signal posts to take an unusual photograph, and even thefts of nameplates, in particular from engine No. 31 *Chale*. A regular annual duty was to open and close Smallbrook Junction signal box.

My boss was very keen on rules and regulations and he asked me to 'stamp out' a regular running practice at Cowes, ie allowing the empty carriage stock to run down the gradient in to the station platform while the locomotive ran around the train. This procedure was blatant rule breaking, Mr Gardener considered. Now, when I visited Cowes station the crews operated by the book, but I know that without exception, while I was absent from the scene every train operated the illegal run-around method, which was an Island railway tradition.

Sometimes I was called to serious railway accidents on the Island railways. One such incident comes to mind at Medina Wharf, during some shunting movements. It is a story that has lessons to be learnt for all those involved with steam locomotives and shunting on today's preserved railways. This particular incident involved a guard riding on the outside of the footplate on the steps of an O2 tank engine. Guard Tom Courtney thought he was safe, but as the locomotive crossed over a point leading into a coal wagon siding his body collided with the end eight-plank wagon. This resulted him being crushed and rolled between locomotive and wagon. When I measured the gap between engine and wagon it was just ten inches! Guard Courtney was lucky to live, but he sustained serious internal injuries.

Shortly before the end of steam on the Island in 1966, following the closure to passenger traffic on the Cowes-Newport-Ryde road, the Locomotive

Operating Department ordered one final massive bulk order of loco coal to take them up to the final end of steam traction. The Southern Region directed all the Island's depots that were closing in the near future, or that had just closed, to dispatch all remaining coal supplies to Ryde St John's Road loco shed for stock piling. Such was the extent of this supply that a vast mountain of coal appeared in front of Ryde shed, providing an unusual spectacle! My task was to ensure that the delivery of these coal supplies from Medina Wharf went according to plan. With the Cowes line closed, a wooden block was gently laid over the rails at Smallbrook Junction and this was removed when any freight traffic ran back and forth. These loco coal trains were literally overloaded with coal so that when the train was in motion much tumbled out on to the lineside. We didn't really bother how much was lost, as the quality was very poor indeed in that some coal came from closed depots where it

had been in store for two or three years already! Our big fear was that having topped Ashey Bank with our heavy weight coal train the wooden block would still be in place. As our forward momentum around the curve could by anything between 30 and 40 mph there would be little to stop us. My instructions to Smallbrook Junction signalmen such as Eddie Spears and Vic Hailes was to always 'give us the road', which was a bit frightening to say the least!

After the end of steam, during the period we were electrifying the Ryde–Shanklin line, Syd Newbury the permanent way inspector, notified me that he had been instructed to remove the connection for the Cowes line at Smallbrook Junction. My thoughts quickly turned to all the redundant steam locomotives stored in Ryde shed. I therefore asked Driver John Townson to steam the best locomotive in order to transfer all these engines, four at a time. As we passed through Haven Street with the first

Lower quadrant signals at Ryde Pier Head, and the water tank immediately behind, provide an ideal stimulus for the Isle of Wight railway modeller.

J. R. G. Griffiths

consignment of O2 tanks in tow behind engine No. 27 *Merstone* hauling at the front end, the legendary Island railway supporter, Miss Winter appeared and gave us a wave. As we approached Wootton station we discovered that there had been an earth slip from the clay embankment, causing some distortion in the track. When the trains ran every day in normal service this problem was regularly cured by the weight of the passage of service trains. I still don't know how we managed to negotiate this problem, but after some slipping we got through. After depositing engines Nos 35, 33, 28 and 22 on the first load we returned to Ryde for our second load; Nos 14, 16, 17 and 20. These were duly dumped in the 'up' bay platform at Newport, on 18th April 1967. An amusing incident occurred on the second journey down. We stopped at Haven Street and gave Miss Winter a footplate ride to Newport and all the way through Wootton

and down Whippingham Bank she muttered "Lovely little engines". I think the last movement was to transfer redundant carriage and wagon stock. The fire was then dropped and it was all over.

During the interim period between the end of steam in December 1966 and the commencement of electric services in April 1967, we retained engines 24 *Calbourne* and 31 *Chale* to assist with works trains. A special ramp was constructed in Ryde St John's yard for the delivery of the underground cars from the mainland via Pickfords lorries. A special match truck was used to pull these electric trailers so that the steam locos could haul them about. On one occasion I thought I would be clever, so I arranged for the third car of the four-carriage electric set to be shunted at the bottom of the ramp, ready to couple up to the fourth carriage which had arrived on the next low loader. As this trailer car was unloaded it broke free and having roller bearings it ran down the ramp and crashed into the waiting stock. This resulted in the whole lot running into the special match truck which

The signalling and point diagram inside Ryde Pier Head signal box, August 1964.

G. M. Kichenside

crumbled between engine 24 and the weight of the electric coach stock! As a result a repair crew had to come down from Acton in London to make good the damage.

Prior to the end of steam the railways were overcrowded on occasions, especially at Ryde Pier Head. I have known passengers obliged to travel in the luggage compartments. Sometimes passengers would complain but nothing was ever put into writing thanks to the good offices of Station Master Bert Smith. Before any complaint had a chance of being made official Bert would take the angry passenger into the Pier Head buffet where they would receive a whisky to calm them down. Hence there were no official written complaints!

On summer Saturdays I would first head out to Sandown on the 7.40am double-header train. Then I would head back to Ryde to wait for trouble – single line token failures, engine failures etc. One day the token failed between Brading and Smallbrook. I was sent to investigate and we discovered that a pheasant had got caught up in the wires. This was quickly cured! On another occasion a storm blew up causing waves to come crashing over the railway pier at Ryde. The wind turned southeasterly. I then had to take a decision when to close the pier to railway traffic. Unfortunately, I left this decision a little too late with a train still up the pier. The sea broke over the pier causing a cable to be detached across the track, obstructing any train movement. I therefore set off on foot with a pair of cutters and rope to either cut the cable or tie it

back. During the process a wave blew over the pier and I was soaked, but the job got done. After seeing the train safely down the pier I took a taxi home to change. The footplate crew shouted to me that if I wanted to have a swim they could bring me some swimming trunks!

One of the most controversial things we used to do on the Island railways in the summer season, was to lock the First Class compartments on the carrriages. The idea here was to prevent the First Class accommodation from being crowded and dirtied by ordinary passengers. On one occasion at Ryde Pier Head someone forgot to lock these compartments and as luck would have it a group of men occupied them. The station foreman challenged these 'gents', who turned out to be the wrestlers Johnny Kwango, Les Kellet, Mick McManus and Steve Logan. They were bound for Ventnor and challenged the station foreman to come in and remove them. He then reported the matter to me. I told him that if he wanted them out, he had better do the job himself!

One of the most frightening experiences in my Island railway duties was to walk through Ventnor Tunnel when steam locomotives were running. I was accompanied by a ganger and it took us about half an hour to walk from one end to the other. It was pitch black and full of smoke fumes from passing trains. In the silence that was broken

No. 35 *Freshwater* on the scissor cross-over at Ryde Pier Head with an 'up' train from Cowes on 31st August 1963.

G. M. Kichenside

RYDE PIER HEAD TRAM STATION – 1935

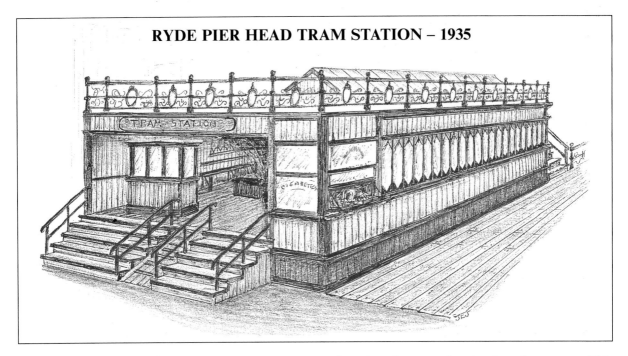

intermittently by drips of water from the brick tunnel walls, I considered how narrow the tunnel was. This fact was brought home to me when a train passed us. At first the ganger informed me that a train had entered the tunnel from the Wroxall end. However, he continued to walk along the sleepers for some two or three minutes before we took cover in the man hole recess in the side wall. The approach of the train could be likened to an approach of an underground train in London. We felt the draft of the air being pushed towards us by the approaching train. The noise was terrific as she passed, and I noted the orange glow from the loco's fire and peered up at the illuminated carriage compartments. The smoke from the O2 tank's chimney then filled our lungs and we feared asphyxiation. Towards the centre of the tunnel, a shaft of light and the passage of fresh air flowed down from above us from a ventilation shaft.

Any shunting of wagons or carriages at Ventnor required shunting movements into the tunnel. The engine would haul stock into the tunnel before setting back to propel it into a given siding. The problem for the loco crew was knowing when the signalman had re-set the points. It was impossible to see a signal from inside the tunnel or look back to the signal box for a flag indication. The footplate crew would therefore listen out for a bell before setting back. Sometimes locomotives hauled their stock too far into the tunnel. Back at Newport I came up with the bright idea of placing colour light markers at set intervals of two, four and six car-

riage lengths to assist the footplate crews. This helped and prevented the signalman having to send someone into the tunnel for a lost train that had gone too far into the tunnel during a shunting movement.

We did experience flooding in Ventnor Tunnel on a few occasions at the Wroxall end. A fresh water stream flowed down the side of the hills and into a culvert. After a heavy down pour this drainage system could not cope with the surge and a flood developed. The water was quite deep across the track causing serious disruption to the service and plenty of problems for Sid Newbury and his P.W. gangers.

Had the Island railways to Ventnor and Cowes remained open today they would without doubt more than pay their way, but with 'steam traction' they would have been a gold mine for British Rail, as busy as any of the preserved railways run by steam enthusiasts.

Island Area Inspectors, 1923–1966, in order of succession:

George Ranger	– Ex-Isle of Wight Central Railway. Retired 1932.
Richard Coker	– Ex-London West Division, Waterloo.
Ernest Gaylord	– Ex-London West Division, Waterloo.
Frank Williams	– Ex-Southern Division, Southampton Central.

George Tanner	–	Ex-London West Division, Woking.
Victor Churchill	–	Ex-London West Division, Waterloo.
Ernest Landon	–	Ex-Isle of Wight Headquarters, Newport.
Henry Powers	–	Ex-London West Division, Woking.
Reginald Piper	–	Ex-London West Division, Wimbledon.
Peter Davridge	–	Ex-London West Division.
Ronald Russell	–	Ex-London West Division, Wimbledon.

Others who covered this position in temporary periods:

Harold Tanner		
George Kingsley	}	All ex-London West Division, Wimbledon.
Harold Kitcher		
Leonard Yarney		
James Hooper	–	Ex-Newport Head Office.

John Wells

Like so many of my colleagues, my railway career started in a predictable way as a Junior at Ryde St John's Road, but I was different in that I was moved to various stations before being called up for National Service in the war. After demob I returned to the railway, rather reluctantly in 1946. For a time I filled in as a passenger guard, but the opportunity presented itself to work in Ryde Pier Head signal box and I seized it.

The Pier Head box was perched perilously above the waters of the Spithead, between the railway pier and the tramway pier. In many respects it was a nice place to work in during the summer as the signalman had an outstanding panoramic view of the sea, and it was possible to watch ocean liners like the *Queen Mary*, *United States* and *France* pass by. In saying this however, we were kept very busy as there were two stations under our control – Pier Head and Esplanade, and there were plenty of train and light engine movements to control. Although we had a good view of the terminal platforms under our control, British Rail did little to encourage safety in steam days, as there was no track circuiting, and the signals were not locked up with block instruments. The only safety measure at our finger tips was a lever collar. The ironic thing was that as soon as the line was electrified and the traffic was minimal they built new safety measures into the Pier Head signal box.

The Pier Head signal box was a potential danger area for possible accidents in steam days. Quite often platform lines would be particularly busy in the Pier Head station and all we had as signalmen to remind us of platform occupation was switches that we had to operate. I suggested installing a 'calling on' signal to the Railway Suggestions Committee, which involved fitting a simple signal arm with a letter 'C' on it. This would inform the driver of 'up' trains that the platform lines he was approaching was partially occupied already. Our system for calling trains to occupied platforms in those days was, to stop them outside the signal box and then display a green hand flag to call them on. At night, we used a hand lamp and the slightest puff of wind and the lamp would be out. Even during the daytime in gales it was almost impossible to wave the flag outside the box. My colleagues in Ryde Pier Head signal box therefore fully supported my 'calling on' signal idea one hundred per cent. The management wrote back and said they were in total support of the idea, but could not impliment it in view of the cost involved.

We also asked for a repeater signal to be built on a dummy signal, as this particular signal often hung in the 'off' position which was extremely dangerous. I pointed this out to an inspector on one occasion and showed him the signal which was stuck in the 'off' position. After banging the culprit signal with my hand it returned to its safe position. It was therefore possible to have a potential accident at any time, but they did not correct the fault.

Occasionally there were incidents at Ryde Pier which happened through no fault of the signalmen. I recall having Inspector Henry Powers up in the box one afternoon and stopping a train to hand signal it and thus carry out the rule procedure as regards platform occupation at Ryde Pier Head. Sometime later I heard that a lady passenger had been injured when the train ran into the platform and hit a van which was being unloaded near the buffer blocks. Apparently, the lady was waiting with the door open as the train drew in to the platform and with the abrupt halt the door slammed back on her.

Even people who should have known better had accidents in the Ryde Pier Head signal box area of control. Obviously, I can only relate stories of those who are not presently employed by British Rail. The classic example involved Inspector Henry Powers. At the time, there was single line working through Ryde Esplanade Tunnel and one of the lines was out of use with no trains working on it at all owing to engineering works. Now, Inspector Powers fully appreciated the situation as he was up inside the Pier Head signal box with me discussing progress on the work being carried out. Henry asked me how long I thought it would take to walk to Ryde St John's Road station and I told him about twenty minutes. I did not dream he would walk along the line through the tunnel. After letting a 'down' train depart Inspector Henry Powers wished me all the best and left the signal box. I was the last man to speak to Inspector Powers as his body was later found in the tunnel. If

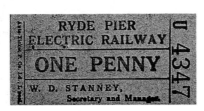

the inspector had wished to walk through the tunnel he should have followed the path of the line out of use. Instead, for some reason, he walked on the line in use and was killed by the passage of a light engine. This man above all men should have known better and I can only assume that he became confused as the light engine approached in the 'S'-shaped Ryde Esplanade Tunnel. This incident shocked me at the time and continues to haunt me to this day.

On some occasions it was impossible to walk down the pier to the signal box because of severely high neep tides. In fact one of my colleagues was stuck up in the box for sometime waiting for low tide on one occasion. The box was open for long periods in steam days owing to the mail trains. We would open at 3am and the mail trains for Cowes and Ventnor would be cleared by 4.15am. There would then be no further trains until about 6am. During this time it was possible for signalmen to do a bit of fishing in the sea below.

When electrification came in 1967, they cut the Pier Head signal box staff down to just two. Although I was the person who had been at this box the longest, since 1950, I was the signalman with least seniority in years of service. Therefore, I was made redundant, along with my faithful companions – the steam engines!

Eric Fry

I spent 49½ years in continuous service on the Isle of Wight railways, apart from a period of absence for war service. I first joined the railway service in April 1936, during the Southern Railway era, starting off as a junior at Ventnor West. Here I remained until being called up to the RAF, but my job was kept open for me until I returned. However, upon my return I was sent initially to Ventnor West then Merstone and Newport until I eventually ended up at the other Ventnor station – Ventnor Town, as it was known. At first I was a porter on the platform, but after getting married I went into the signal box. In 1958, I transferred as a Grade Three signalman to Ryde Pier Head and here I stayed until the end of steam. In saying this however, I did have to spend a few months out at Newchurch owing to some 'railway red tape'. It

Ready for action, Signalman Eric Fry at Ryde Pier Head signal box waits for the next train movement in August 1964.

G. M. Kichenside

Signalman Eric Fry stands in front of his signal box at Ryde Pier Head while up in the box, looking out of the window, is Shunter H. Jim Yeo.
H. J. Yeo Collection

Signalman Eric Fry has just been relieved from the early turn of duty at Ryde Pier Head signal box and can be observed walking down the catwalk alongside the railway. This unique photograph was taken from the inner home signal which Island railway enthusiasts will remember as the signal post which also carried the route indicator. An O2 tank waits to depart from Ryde Pier Head with a train for Newport and Cowes. The signal box is clearly visible, and to the left, are the two parallel lines of the Pier tramway while a Volkswagen Beetle can be seen proceeding along the roadway of Ryde Pier.
Ron H. Childs

The king is in his castle – Signalman Eric Fry at work in Ryde Pier Head signal box.

G. M. Kichenside

Opposite: **Horse Boat Slipway (Adjoining Ryde Esplanade station)**

During the 1920s cattle and horses were transported to the mainland in flat bottomed barges towed across by a steam tug. On arrival at Ryde the tug would release its tow close inshore and seaman would guide the barges to the slipway with the aid of long poles. The fact that horse traffic was predominantly carried on in the early years probably explains how the slipway became known as "Horse Boat Slipway"; but as it could only be used at high water and as motor traffic increased it was eventually abandoned and the Southern transferred all its activities to Fishbourne where better facilities were available. Before the transfer however, scenes such as are depicted here were typical of the arrival of the "Horse Boat" on one of its not too frequent visits.

was discovered that the young lad at Newchurch, Roy Pointer, was working the levers at only a few months under the age of 18. As soon as they found this out I had to swap places with him and he took my job at Ventnor on a temporary basis.

Mention of my short period at Newchurch, brings back sad memories of watching the first batch of children to arrive for wartime evacuation. They arrived, tired, frightened, and loaded with suitcases. Further up the line at Merstone there was a signalman in those days called Harold Blundy. He was very proud of his signal box and everything had to be cleaned and polished – every gauge, lever, clock and so on. He went so far as to wash out the coal bucket and even to washing the coal before it went in the bucket!

During the period of time I was at Ryde Pier Head signal box, a shunter dropped an Annett's key into the sea under the box. Now this key was a vital piece of apparatus as it locked up the frame. Luckily, Cyril Henley and his colleagues from the Signal & Telegraph Department were on hand and they helped me work the box for an hour, while I tried to recover it. At first they came out in a boat and searched to no avail. Then we got a magnet on a piece of line and luckily it picked up the Annett's key and no more was said about it.

There was one driver you had to be careful of at Ryde Pier and that was Driver 'Mad' Jack Sturgess. Now the signal box was provided with a coke burner and the signalman on the middle turn of duty used to go and collect a bucket of coke from the station. I vividly recall leaving a bucket of coke at the end of the platform one day for a few minutes while I went to the refreshment room. When I returned the smiling face of Driver Sturgess greeted me from the footplate of his engine No. 22 *Brading.* Thinking no more I carried that bucket back to the box, but it seemed to be heavier than ever. It wasn't until I reached the signal box that I discovered why the bucket was so much heavier. Apparently, while the bucket was left unattended, 'Mad' Jack had used his engine peep pipe to half fill the bucket with water. Next time, I was wise to Mr Sturgess and his tricks.

On arriving for duty one day at 1pm, I saw the most curious sight of my railway career. It was a foggy day and I could not see the starting signals until 7 o'clock that night. Because it was so foggy they cancelled the Ryde–Portsmouth boat service. The queue began to build up down the pier as each train arrived at Ryde Pier Head station, until at the end of the day the queue stretched from Ryde Pier Head to Ryde Esplanade pier gates. It was decided

HORSE BOAT SLIPWAY – RYDE c.1923

therefore to detrain passengers at Ryde Esplanade, so that they could join the queue. They waited out there for almost six hours until the fog cleared and the boats resumed service again.

There was one occasion on which I had a derailment occur on the pier section which disrupted the smooth running of the service for some four hours. Driver Denny Snow took water on his O2 tank at the end of platform 2 and ran forward to the crossover point where the engine waited for clearance to run back on to the end of its train, which was waiting back in the platforms. Meanwhile, I pulled the signals for a train to proceed up the pier from Ryde Esplanade to run into platform 1. The points were set for the approaching 'up' train and I then pulled the inner home signal. Now at this point, Driver Snow's engine moved back across the crossover points and became derailed. How the confusion for the light engine to move forward came about I don't know. What I do know is that we had single line working 'up' and 'down' the pier, with trains working in to platforms 3 and 4 only. A flag man helped me with signals while the engine was put back on the road.

It was a very busy signal box in steam days, particularly on Summer Saturdays when the service consisted of one train an hour each way on the Newport and Cowes road; two trains each way to and from Ventnor; one each way as far as Shanklin, and one each way as far as Sandown. To recap, that is five arrivals and five departures each hour! Even the normal hourly Winter Timetable routine was quite complex at Ryde Pier Head box. The boat would arrive from Portsmouth Harbour at five minutes past the hour. Waiting in platform 2 ready with a locomotive would be a train for Newport and Cowes and alongside her, in platform 1, would be a set of coaches for Ventnor, but with no engine at the front yet. At 13 minutes past the hour, a train would arrive in platform 3 from Cowes. At 18 minutes past the hour the train for Newport and Cowes in platform 2 would depart. As soon as this train was clear I would then get the locomotive in platform 3 to run forward to the blocks, pull the dummy signal and she would back over the crossover points on to the now vacant adjacent road, and out as far as my Pier Head signal box. The engine would then back down and couple on to the train for Ventnor in platform 1. By this time the train from Ventnor would be arriving and running into platform 4 at 21 minutes past the hour. four minutes later, the train for Ventnor on platform 1 would leave. After this hectic period things would quieten down and I could watch the boat leave at

RYDE PIER ENTRANCE – 1935

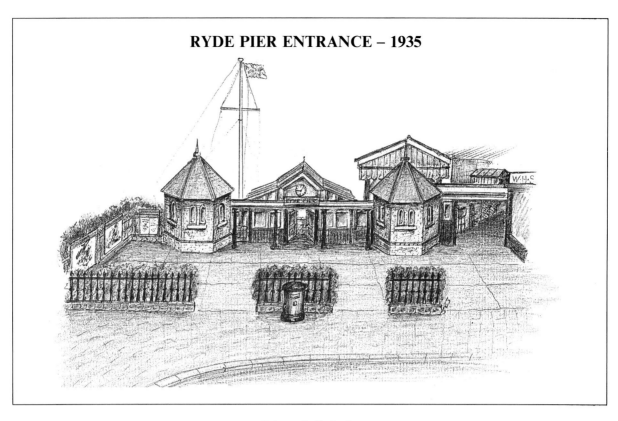

Gateway to England.

half past the hour, and yes, it was possible to see a paddle steamer on this service right up to the end of steam!

Back to business in the signal box, the next requirement in the hourly routine in winter was to get the locomotive locked in platform 4 to shunt its train out of the station, and then push it, after running around into platform 1 in readiness for the next boat arrival. This engine would then run light to St John's Road depot for coaling and servicing. Roughly on the stroke of the hour another locomotive would run in 'light engine' from St John's Road depot and shunt the carriage set in platform 3 into platform 2 for the next train to Newport and

Cowes. Thus the hourly winter routine would start all over again. Now if you think that was a mouthfull, and hard work pulling all those levers in the box, try thinking about operating the Pier Head box on a Summer Saturday!

The Pier Head signal box somehow managed to survive electrification, but sadly it was not long before it was closed and it is sad to see it gone when I go up Ryde Pier today. As for me, well I moved on to Sandown signal box and ended my railway service there. Today, I often enjoy nostalgic railway discussions with my brother Harold who used to work in Ventnor signal box, but that's another story.

Driver Cyril Eason's view from the spectacle of No. 33 *Bembridge* at Ryde Esplanade station on 2nd May 1963.

Dr John Mackett

Left: **Driver Harry 'Toby' Watson JP looks out from the cab of No. 16 *Ventnor* as it approaches Ryde Esplanade with a train for Ventnor on 29th August 1964. In the foreground is the Esplanade cross-over which is worked from the ground frame seen in between the lines. This ground-frame was released from the Pier Head signal box.**

G. M. Kichenside

Driver Eddie Prangnell's No. 21 *Sandown* waits to leave Ryde Esplanade with a train for Ventnor. *Peter J. Relf*

Ryde Esplanade was always the busiest commuter station in the Island, mainly because of mainland traffic. At one time there were as many as ten licensed outside porters conveying passengers' luggage to all parts of the town, and probably twenty or so taxis on the ranks outside of the station.

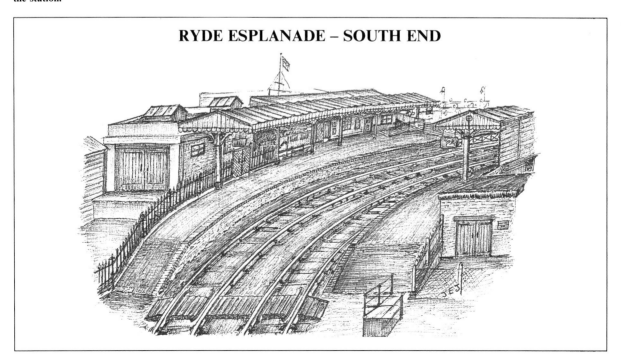

RYDE ESPLANADE – SOUTH END

RYDE ST JOHN'S ROAD

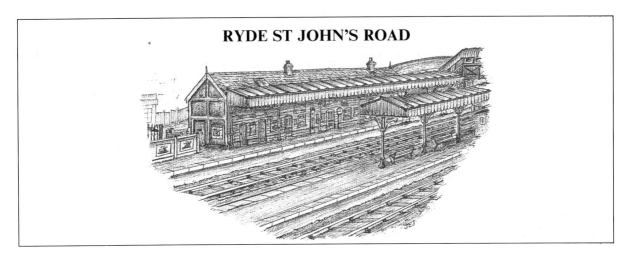

The layout of Ryde St John's Road was altered many times over the years, through expansion of space and staff, through the reduction of both of these things, for economic reasons, and through electrification. After the electrification scheme was completed, St Johns lost its complement of freight and goods wagons, plus the extensive shunting yard. Its engine sheds were demolished, and the loss of all these things seemed to be the severance of the last link between steam and electricity.

The LCGB "Farewell to Isle of Wight Steam" special leaving Ryde Esplanade on a wrong line working to Ryde St John's Road and thence to Shanklin, and return. The special left Ryde Esplanade at 12.15pm in heavy rain, but the sun broke out for the return 'up' working some two hours later. The train was double-headed by Nos 31 *Chale* and 24 *Calbourne* and banked through Ryde Tunnel by No. 17 *Seaview*. *Chale* was driven by Gerald Coombes and fired by Dave "Jed Clampett" Rendell, *Calbourne* was driven by Doug Saunders and fired by Johnnie Howe with the train's guard being Jack Tharme, whilst at the rear *Seaview* was driven by Jim Hunnybun.

Peter J. Relf

Joe H. Russell

My railway career had humble beginnings as a junior parcel porter at Ryde St John's Road in 1930, and I retired in January 1981 as Area Manager of Dover Area on the South Eastern Division of British Rail Southern Region. The staff that I remember at Ryde St John's Road almost half a century ago were: Station Master Mr Malcolm Buckett, who went to Southampton Terminus as traffic controller; in the ticket office were Charlie Reeves and Gordon Corbett, the station foreman was Harry Philips – known to everyone as 'Benny' Philips. There were two porters: Alfie Simmonds, who smoked a cherry wood pipe constantly, and Bill Lynett who always had a Woodbine cigarette in his mouth. In the parcels office were Lesley Anderson and myself. The signal box at St John's in those days was manned by three signalmen: Bill Ward, George Lambert and Vic Lacey, senior. We also had a lampman, Toby Hailes, who quite surprisingly was almost lame. This job must have been a hard graft for Toby as it was dangerous and involved much climbing up signals ladders, but he somehow managed it.

As the junior parcel porter at St John's Road, my duties involved plodding on foot all around the yard, collecting the wagon numbers. The freight traffic was very busy and included coal for the loco shed, local traders and merchants, and for the gasworks, and various mixed freight. After collecting details of wagon numbers and loads, my next task was to write out advice notes for each and deliver them around Ryde. In addition to this there were parcels to deal with and PLA or 'passenger luggage in advance'. We were also responsible for ticket collections at St John's Road. Tickets not only had to be collected, but be sorted out into number order and then bundled up and sent off to the audit department. If we were any tickets short a letter would be sent demanding to know what had happened to them.

One curious thing struck me immediately in those days about the destinations from which trains at St John's Road had come from or were going to. The trains going to or arriving from Newport and Cowes were always referred to as, "The Central train arriving is the . . .". Likewise, trains destined for the Ventnor and Shanklin line were always announced as, "The Isle of Wight

No. 24 *Calbourne* enters Ryde St John's Road with a train for Ventnor, and as subsequent pictures taken by the same photographer reveal, the driver was Nelson Parsons with fireman Terry Drudge.

Peter J. Relf

train....". The reason for this later became clear as there had been two separate railway companies operating these lines prior to 1923, the Isle of Wight Central Railway and the Isle of Wight Railway. Staff always knew from which line trains were coming, even in Southern days, as trains from the Ventnor line would give advance notice of their arrival by blowing two long blasts on their engine whistles on passing Smallbrook, whereas the Cowes trains would give just one long whistle.

Perhaps the most unusual traffic we dealt with, which is not usually associated with the Isle of Wight, was pigeons for Ryde Pigeon Club. To begin with we sent the baskets of pigeons just across the water to Portsmouth for release by the station staff there. Later we sent them to Guildford and further afield, until in the end they were sent up to Banff Harbour in Scotland, prior to the 'News Of The World' Race. Apparently, all the birds arrived back in Ryde safely.

Each week cattle would arrive at St John's Road travelling via the cattle boat at Ryde Esplanade. They would then be loaded aboard cattle wagons that had been shunted specially into the 'up' platform and dispatched to various parts of the Island railway system. My colleague, Les Anderson, and myself decided one day that the station foreman should be herded into the former LBSCR cattle wagons with some of the beasts and this we managed to achieve. Furthermore, in our skylarking about we also succeeded in placing a shovel full of cattle manure under the mat in 'Benny' Philips' office. The station foreman smelt this fragrant perfume and attempted to discover its source. Having got away with our first deposit of steaming brown manure, we then set out to deliver a second shovel full under our station foreman's mat. Little did we know that Mr Philips was laying in wait for us to walk into his trap! When he caught us – well, all I can say is our heads were sore.

Twice a year Les Anderson and myself were released from all duties for a mail check. Our object was to count every mail bag and parcel that arrived at Ryde Pier to make sure the Post Office was not overcharging. This was a duty to look forward to each six months as we had to travel with the mail to Ventnor or Cowes. Often, mail being loaded at St John's Road was so great that they would throw us on top of the mountain of mail bags to ascertain how much there was. Let us suppose there were six mail bags bound for London, five would have round collars on them but the sixth would have a square collar with a number written on it, showing how many bags were in the consignment. This would then be entered up in our special notebooks.

At one time there was an air service between Portsmouth and Ryde. The aeroplanes that operated this service would land at the old Ryde Airport which was located at Westridge Cross. The Southern Railway were interested to know whether to acquire this service. The railway authorities selected a young parcel porter from Sandown, by the name of Ron Anderson to lurk about in the lane outside the airport and do a bit of spying for them. His assignment was to observe and record all landings of aircraft on this service, make a note of the passengers alighting and joining the aircraft, and assess the amount of luggage conveyed. With these figures to hand Ron was then sent to the General Post Office in Union Street, Ryde each night where he sent a telegram to the Superintendent at Woking, Southern Railway Offices.

As the time for Ron Anderson's booked annual leave approached, the local authorities on the railways selected me to take over this special assignment during his absence. I did not know which were the special planes to be observed at Ryde Airport as I could not tell one plane from another. Ron reassured me that things would be all right and promised to point out the special aeroplanes to me on the Monday morning. Unfortunately, when Monday morning arrived Ron was nowhere to be seen. I therefore obtained copies of the previous week's figures and averaged them out. Each day could then be spent on more serious matters, such as blackberry picking and appreciating the countryside around the airport. No one ever questioned my figures and I suppose that in a small way I contributed to the Southern Railway purchasing the airline. In saying this, the air service was doomed to failure as the airfield at Ryde was so far out and off the beaten track, that passengers had to rely on taxis, thus little time was actually saved!

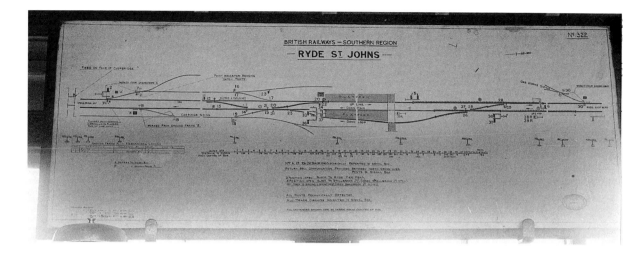

Ryde St John's Road signal box track diagram in May 1962.
H. P. Mason

A common sight in those days at Ryde St John's Road was a horse and carriage, known as a horse omnibus. The owner was known as, 'Betsy Life' and he used to sit out in the station yard and wait for trade from passengers alighting from the trains. He used to wait out there with his whip and drop off to sleep with his horse. If and when passengers required a lift they would climb into the carriage and shout out where they wanted to be taken. One day my colleague, Les Anderson, went out into the station yard and jumped in and said, "Number One, Great Preston Road, please." Betsy woke up and proceeded as instructed. It wasn't until half way up Oakfield Hill that he realised just who his passenger was. He chucked Les Anderson out there and then with a size nine boot behind him!

Mr R. W. Kemp refers to the daily time signal sent out from Newport, on page 104 of *Once Upon a Line... Volume Two*, and I can confirm that this same omnibus telephone system operated on the Island railway system during my era at St John's Road in the thirties. It was possible to communicate with any station on the Isle of Wight, but the disadvantage was that only one conversation could be held at any one time. If staff wished to make a telephone call, they were obliged to pick up the telephone and enquire if it was engaged. It was possible for anyone to listen into a telephone conversation, and they frequently did! Therefore, one got to know the names and voices of staff throughout the Isle of Wight railways.

The railway used to convey a lot of goods for a local street trader called Ernie Hewitson. By this I mean fruit, nuts and whatever was in season. He had a very persuasive way with him and a good voice to announce his wares that were for sale. I remember that he would quite often receive two crates of fish via the railway, fresh from Grimsby or

Hull. After unloading it from the train, I would assist Ernie in loading the fish onto his barrow. He would then push the barrow out on to the main road, and as soon as he turned into Monkton Street, Mr Hewitson would call out, "Fresh fish for sale. Sandown Bay herring straight from the net!"

Times were hard in the 1930s and we were always on the lookout for something for nothing on the railways. This came in the form of free cigarettes from a passenger who was a bookmaker. He would travel from St John's Road to his office at Sandown on four days per week. This bookmaker, named Mr Boynton, would return later in the day 'well oiled', being a gentleman that appreciated his liquor. His favourite brand of cigarette was Ardath which gave away coupons. If you were on the ticket barrier Mr Boynton would give you a packet of this brand of cigarettes. Word soon spread if Dickie Boynton, the bookmaker was on the train. Some artful railway characters would meet him off the 'up' train and greet him by name. They would then receive their free packet of cigarettes. Their next move would be to run through the parcels office and be on the ticket barrier in time to collect their second packet!

In those days the Isle of Wight railways were staffed by young men with little spare money to spend on entertainment, so they used to have fun at work and yarn to our colleagues who became trusted friends. Sometimes our horseplay caught up with us as the following anecdote relates. There was a grade one porter at Bembridge called Charlie Wetherick who had the reputation of being rather short tempered and it seemed to be everybody's duty to torment the poor fellow. My friend Ron

28

Anderson from Sandown acquired an apple box one day, filled it up with ballast from between the sleepers on the line and addressed it to Charlie at Bembridge station. The box duly arrived via the branch train from Brading, and Charlie did not take too kindly to his present. Upon closer examination he discovered an old label on the box and was able to track down the culprit. He then reported the incident in full to the authorities on the railway, who fined Ron Anderson the carriage for the parcel from Sandown to Bembridge, which was about a quarter of his wages! So this proved that 'he who laughs last, laughs longest'!

There used to be a tremendous number of street sellers in those days, as there were no supermarkets and few cars to transport shopping. People would specialise in selling certain items and one such street seller was the fishmonger Margie Cotton, who regularly travelled from St John's Road to Brading, with his barrow, fish and weights. One day he travelled down to Brading as usual and left

his weights on the train in the guard's van. The station staff promptly notified Sandown station that, Margie Cotton had left his weights on the train and asked if they could be sent back on the next 'up' train. In those days there was a popular brand of cigarette called Waites, and so Sandown station staff phoned back to say they could not find any cigarettes. Poor Margie lost half his day's trade over that affair.

The structure of promotion in those days was that one completed your time as a junior at the age of 18. It was the practice for the 18-year old junior to then be sent for the summer season to Wroxall where a third member of staff was required to help out during the Summer Timetable. At the end of the Summer Timetable, the last week of September, the promoted employee would then be found a new post away from St John's Road and Wroxall. My predecessor was Roy Way and he followed this pattern, firstly to Wroxall and thence I believe, to Newchurch. During the summer that Roy was away at Wroxall I was only temporary at St John's Road, but when Roy was appointed to Newchurch they offered me a permanent position. I was told by

An interior view of Ryde St John's Road signal box.
J. R. G. Griffiths

the chief clerk at Newport "If you behave yourself my son, you'll be on the permanent staff." I never forgot this comment until I retired, when they did eventually get rid of me, some 50 years later.

On completion of my time at Ryde St John's Road, I was sent to Yarmouth as a porter, conveying luggage to and from the station to the pier and slipway. It was a dreadful job that had to be done in all weathers, but somehow I stuck it out. Now the porters on the pier were not railway porters, but were employed by Yarmouth Town Trust. There was great rivalry between us as they carried purely passengers' luggage and thereby had all the tips, whereas we had to carry all the passenger luggage in advance, camp gear, fruit and fish. Eventually, the grade one porter in the ticket office was firstly on sick leave and I was sent to cover his job. Then, as luck would have it, this fellow left and I got his job after some time. Whilst at Yarmouth, I

got married and so every penny then counted, and once again I had to seek promotion – this time to Brading.

Brading station was a busy little place in those days, as it was the junction for St Helens and Bembridge, but foremost it was the first station out of Ryde on the main line to Ventnor. Whilst based here, I was the grade one porter in the ticket office, but this job had a little perk of an extra half-a-crown payment per week for operating the water pump on the locomotive water tank on the Brading–Bembridge branch. Also, every other Sunday throughout the summer season it was possible to earn some overtime pay, which made a considerable difference to our standard of living. The station had quite a staff at the time: Station Master Stan Martin, Signalman Roy Way, Signalman Alf Cammell, Porter-Signalman Vic Hailes, Porter George Frampton, plus two guards attached

Stretch, Bill! Signalman Bill Day hands the single line token for St John's Road to Brading to the driver of a Shanklin bound train on 30th December 1966.

Brian Stephenson

Opposite page: **No. 30** *Shorwell* **departs from Ryde St John's Road, bunker-first, with a train for Cowes.**
J. R. G. Griffiths

to the station staff for the Bembridge branch services – Walter Buckett and Alf Galimore. One would never believe that so many worked at Brading station if you saw it today. It wasn't long before Signalman Alf Cammell left the box and emigrated to Australia. The opportunity thus arose for me to become a signalman in Brading box and my application was successful.

During the summer season, especially on Saturdays, things were exceptionally busy at Brading. Signalman Roy Way and myself went on to overtime, as Porter-Signalman Vic Hailes was sent to work out at Smallbrook Junction for the season. There was one consolation in that we were provided with a runner to collect and dispatch the single line tokens, which made life easier. Under my control in Brading box was the double-track section to Sandown, the single line to Smallbrook Junction and of course the single line to St Helens and Bembridge. A train would arrive from Bembridge roughly every 30 minutes and there were quite a lot of movements with levers to pull. To get the train in to Brading, I would have to pull levers 17 and 21, and replace those. Next, the locomotive would require to run around its train and levers 14, 10, 8 and 9 would be pulled to take the engine up to

the Bembridge end of its train. Finally, levers 17 and 21 would be pulled to return the locomotive to its train. This was quite hard work every half an hour, bearing in mind that movements had to be recorded in the Train Register as well.

Although I was based at Brading, I still continued to make acquaintance with staff at other Island stations. Perhaps the person I felt sorry for most was old Harry Bishop who worked on his own at Ashey station. This poor fellow had been a shunter for most of his railway career, but unfortunately lost his arm in an accident. With one arm it was impossible for Harry to cycle back home to Daniel Street in Ryde after the last train had gone. He was therefore restricted to walking to and from work. In those days Ashey station had gas lamps and it was quite a struggle for the one-armed Harry to climb a ladder and light these lamps in high winds holding the box of matches in his teeth. Even worse was the fact that Harry had to hump around 2 cwt sacks of chicken feed off trains. It was a pitiful sight.

There was one guard who used to pass through Brading who was rather jinxed, as he would sometimes be left behind on the platform, especially when Driver Jack Sturgess on engine No. 22

Brading was at the front. This guard was none other than, Tom Courtney. Wherever there was trouble, whether it be a train off the road or some other problem, Tom would be there. One night we had some carriages off at Brading on the Chalk Siding. Just as this mess was being cleared away, the freight arrived at Brading from St John's Road, and its guard was, Tom Courtney. He shouted up to me in the box, rather confidently, "Evening Joe. This accident on the Chalk Siding is one that they can't blame on me." With a smile and a wave I watched Tom set off to St Helens and Bembridge peering over the verandah of his ex-London & South Western road van. Thirty minutes passed and all was silent in Brading box. Then suddenly, the telephone went, "It's Tom Courtney here at St Helens, we've got a derailment here!" Such was Tom's extraordinary bad luck.

For three successive Sundays thereafter we had derailments at St Helens Quay. It was surprising how everyone 'mucked in' and got the trains back on the rails on each occasion, but this was just typical of the Isle of Wight railways in those days.

One incident I will never forget is when my good friend, George Wright (who replaced Les Anderson at St John's Road) was hit by an 'up' train. What's more he survived. He was working at Ryde St John's Road and was going to take some letters from the parcel's office to a 'down' train to Ventnor. He ran out of the parcels office and decided to cross the line. At that precise moment an 'up' train headed by an O2 tank was approaching. The locomotive hit him on the buttock and he was thrown in under the coping of the platform and survived.

Being married to an engine driver's daughter one got to know quite a lot about other amusing incidents on the Island lines. My father-in-law was Driver Jack Elliot and his regular engine was No. 18 *Ningwood.* One day he arrived at Ryde Pier Head aboard engine 18 with his regular fireman Bill Drake, some minutes late. They were both spoken to rather harshly by Guard Bill Skinner about the loss of time. They decided to run around the train in the platforms and couple up as soon as possible. The plan was that as soon as the guard waved his green flag, the regulator would be opened fully and they would leave Guard Skinner behind. Sure enough the green flag was waved and the engine crew set off at full speed on their O2 tank. Half way down the pier my father-in-law noticed that their train was still in the platforms at Ryde Pier Head. They had to return, red faced, to hear more angry words from their guard.

Finally, a passenger once asked me whether I

knew that the Island railways were mentioned in the Bible. He quoted the following verse from the book of Genesis, ". . . and was created every creeping thing that crept along the face of the earth." At the time I didn't think this was amusing, but after I left the Island railways in 1953 I could look back and laugh.

Les Anderson

My family came over to the Isle of Wight in 1919, as my father worked on the permanent way between Ryde Pier Head and Ryde St John's Road for the London & South Western Railway. The first time I came over to the Island was on a paddle steamer with my mother. My father had to travel separately, accompanying our luggage on a tug-hauled barge between Portsmouth and Ryde Esplanade. Funnily enough we passed my father mid-way across the Spithead.

It followed that I should work on the Island railways when old enough and I started as an office boy junior at Ryde CME Works, under the reign of the Southern Railway in 1926. I worked in this position for two years and my job involved looking after three offices, checking staff timesheets and being a general dog's body running here, there, and everywhere. My daily routine at Ryde Works commenced just before 7.15am each morning by making ready the Works' staff brass identification tags. These would be handed out to the staff as they arrived for duty each day. The Works' bell would be rung at precisely 7.30am to indicate the start of work and if any member of the staff was not through the entrance by the time the bell had stopped, he would not be allowed to start work until half an hour later.

It was when I worked at Ryde Works that I was first introduced to the Southern Railway official method of making copies of written documents and letters. Looking back from the present day of photocopying by the mere push of a button, to those far off days of the 1920s when not even carbon paper was in use, one wonders how we ever managed. The primitive method of making copies involved using copying ink, dampening a special copying book and using a press. One needed a lot of luck to obtain a perfect copy. There were always activities to cause amusement during the mundane clerical duties whilst working in Ryde Works. I vividly remember observing Bill Smith who was later to become Works Chargehand Foreman, climbing up on to the roof of the Works as an escapade. I watched him carefully tip paraffin down a chimney for a mischievous joke on his boss who was working down below. As he made his retreat back to his work bench across the roof, poor Bill had the misfortune to slip down through a sky light. He landed unhurt – right in front of his boss!

In those days the staff at Ryde Works were a friendly bunch and I recall that it was Mr Urie, the Superintendent, who took me down to Ryde sea front to teach me how to drive a motor car. The Works Foreman, Bob Sweetman, bought a Morris Cowley car with an old fashioned fold back hood and a 'sit up and beg' type seat arrangement. He was so proud of his new car, and after her first week on the Island roads Mr Sweetman asked me to polish the paint work. Now, in order to give the front of the vehicle a mirror finish I had to back the car up. As I reversed across the Works Yard I heard a dreadful crunching sound at the rear of the car. After climbing to examine what had happened my worst fears were confirmed – I had reversed into a pile of steam locomotive boiler tubes. The damage was so extensive that even the upholstery inside the car was damaged. The Works staff saw what had happened and took pity on me. Coppersmith Chiverton, Painter Rodwell and their assistants set to and repaired Mr Sweetman's car, so that it looked as good as new. This action was just typical of the spirit of railwaymen generally on the Island railways in those days.

After two years in the Works, I transferred to the Operating Department as a junior porter at Wootton. Wootton station was an interesting place to work at in those days. It was situated on the Ryde–Newport line, between Haven Street and Whippingham, with one platform on the 'up', or north, side of the line. I guess it was unusual in design in that staff accommodation and the booking office were located beneath the arch of the adjacent road bridge. The permanent way ganger was always encountering problems with the embankment opposite and the platform, which was formed of clay. After heavy rain this clay would quite often slip onto the railway line, creating delays to the service. After two years I transferred back to Ryde St John's Road station which was about seven miles up the line.

I was to work at St John's Road station for the next 15 years except for a short spell of absence working at Yarmouth station. My duties were mainly centred around the booking office and parcels office where I made many good friends during the course of my work. With no television and little spare money to spend on entertainments, we made our own entertainment at work with practical jokes. One day I managed to trick a

Les Anderson missed his vocation when he entered the Railway Service :—

colleague, Joe Russell, into going up into the roof above the station on the pretext of searching for a lost item of equipment. As soon as poor Joe was safely up through the trap door entrance we sealed the opening, leaving Joe in complete darkness. He wandered around the rafters shouting, "Let me out! Let me out!". Eventually the Station Foreman, Benny Philips, let Joe down.

We all liked to visit St John's signal box when time permitted, to chat to Signalman Lacey. He was rather partial to sweets and this was his downfall, for we decided to give him some Bona-mints. Tasting like spearmints, the good signalman must have eaten almost a whole packet of these Bonamints in between pulling the signal and point levers. Little did Signalman Lacey realise that these sweets were actually a laxative. The staff on the station waited and watched for signs of action in the box and sure enough, later in the day frequent visits were made to the W.C.

Before the Second World War there were the famous Schneider Trophy air races around the Solent and Spithead. Ryde Pier and sea front would be packed with spectators keenly watching the race and every possible advantage would be taken by railway staff of exploiting vantage points located on railway property. Bets would be exchanged between railwaymen on possible winners and reports were relayed throughout the railway network via the internal telephone lines. Jim Attrill had the bright idea of observing the air race from the top of Ryde St John's Road 'up' repeater signal. This was by far the tallest signal on the Isle of Wight railways and come the day of the race it was packed with railway staff who had a unique and wonderful panoramic view across Ryde and the Spithead. The lattice signal began to sway back and forth. Whether this was the wind or the weight of the bodies I will never know, suffice to say that we all visited the toilet on our decent!

During the War I was based at St John's Road. I recall the day when the Luftwaffe's bombers came across, dropping bombs on Ryde. I remember that one bomb fell on the railway yard at St John's Road, damaging O2 tank No.16 *Ventnor*, at the chimney end of the locomotive. The bomb also wrecked a railway carriage. Luckily no humans were killed, but my pet canary bird was killed in the air raid. This incident really brought home to me that there was a war on!

I joined the Railway Home Guard at Ryde and my regular turn of duty was to patrol the railway line up to Smallbrook Junction with colleague Jim Attrill. One moonlit night Jim had the bright idea to climb over a fence for some apples in an orchard that backed on to the railway line. Minutes after Jim set off on his raid into the orchard, there was a German air raid. Suddenly, several Junkers and Heinkel planes flew low over my head and headed towards Portsmouth Dockyards. Shortly afterwards I heard the sound of hob-nailed boots approaching. Could it be some German fifth columnists who had parachuted in? Could it be the farmer who had spotted Jim? I hailed Jim to return immediately with his scrumped apples. He leapt over that wooden fence and we hid under Smallbrook Bridge out of sight. We peered up to see who it was in such a hurry and to our surprise we saw an old horse which had bolted in fright at the sound of the German aircraft.

In those days we were all very proud of our boys in the RAF. We would dash out of the station to observe our Spitfire and Hurricane fighters in action. One day the staff at St John's Road station paused in their railway duties to look up to the skies above and watch a few Spitfires fly over on a training flight. To our horror we witnessed two of them touch accidently. Sadly, both aircraft spun down to earth out of control and crashed next to the railway line. People forget nowadays just what a price those gallant young boys who were pilots in the RAF paid for our freedom.

With so many people called up to serve in the armed forces, hairdressers were few and far between. I therefore took up being the 'railway hairdresser' and I have even walked out to Smallbrook Junction signal box to cut Signalman Ron Haile's hair. One day I decided to have a bit of fun and cut one chap's hair on one side only! The poor man didn't know what to do with himself. I left him in this state for a day, but took pity and finished the other side the following day.

Before and after the War, a regular sight at certain times of the year was the visiting Frenchmen on their bicycles who went around the Island selling onions. They would arrive at Cowes, where I sometimes served and we would store their baskets of onions at Cowes station. They would then set off with strings of onions around their necks on their characteristic bikes. Sadly, this is a sight that has disappeared, just like Cowes station.

During the summer season we also had foreign visitors from Italy who came to the Island to entertain the tourists on Ryde Pier and sea front.

Les Anderson at work in the booking office of Ryde St John's Road station.

Les Anderson

They would play barrel organs from morning to night, and make a small fortune in the process. These barrel organs would be stored in Ryde St John's Road station parcels office prior to the commencement of the season. The Italian barrel organists would remove the handles from the barrel organs to prevent them being played, but the railway staff soon learnt that they could be played by inserting a ticket clipper and revolving it like a handle. Quite often the station at St John's Road would ring out in the morning with the sound of barrel organ music. One particular morning Jim Attrill decided to have a go on his favourite barrel organ in between train services, but just as he started to play, who should walk in to the station but the owner of this very instrument! The small dark haired Italian gentleman stared in disbelief and shouted, "The blood-u-t-sauce! I get you the blood-u-t-sack!" Seeing how potentially serious the situation was for Jim, I tried to defuse the argument by apologising prefusely and saying it would never happen again. The hot-blooded Italian gentleman began to mellow and eventually calmed down.

Whenever something of a musical flavour came into St John's parcels office, there was always a railwayman who would have a go at trying it out. Once we had a one-string fiddle arrive off a train ready to be collected by a local person. Minutes after placing it onto the shelf Signalman Sid Sartin spotted it and promptly removed it to play, "God Save The King". Unfortunately, the string snapped and I began to worry about its imminent collection. I therefore left Sid to look after the parcels office, while I went out to the local music shop for a replacement string. Here I was offered a variety of different strings each for different notes. I think I picked a 'G' string and promptly placed it in the fiddle. I often wonder if the owner was ever any the wiser.

Sid Sartin was an unusual signalman in that while he worked in the signal boxes at Ryde and later Ventnor, he would amuse himself in between duties by embroidering various items for home. He had a lively sense of humour and he would look out for a certain lady who was deaf to enter St John's station. He would suddenly appear in the ticket office seconds before the lady approached. He would then take a back seat and observe the proceedings. She would come up to the ticket office and place her ear trumpet through the hole in the glass partition. This was in the days before National Health Service hearing aids, of course. Sid would then smile as he watched the deaf lady and myself enter into a noisy conversation about the destinations and times of trains. After deciding

on which train, a fight would then develop in feeding the ticket and money past the ear trumpet. Such was life working at St John's station ticket office!

Quite often Ryde Works had to send items of equipment away to Eastleigh Works for repair as there was too much to repair in the small workshops at Ryde. On one occasion Bob Sweetman brought over a boxed up locomotive Westinghouse brake pump to St John's parcels office, which was to be sent by train to Eastleigh Works. At the time of delivery our parcels office was stacked high with passenger luggage in advance and so the pump was stored on a rack at the top until there was a convenient moment for dispatch. However, Jim Attrill and myself promptly forgot all about it and it remained there for some three months! Meanwhile Foreman Sweetman kept on asking when was his pump going to arrive back. Eventually Jim discovered the lost pump and promptly dispatched it on the next train. A week later the repaired pump returned to Ryde, but Bob vowed he would never send anything else to Eastleigh Works.

Not long before I came to St John's Road the whole structure of the station was extensively altered by the Southern Railway in 1927/28. The original platform on the west side of the line became the 'up' platform for all trains, whereas the Island platform which had been used by 'up' and 'down' trains on the Ventnor line services became the 'down' main and loop platforms. Looking up under the station verandah at St John's, it was possible to see the names of each station on the line cast into the supporting pillar structuring. Whilst walking along the 'down' island platform one day I peered into the First Class compartments of a Ventnor bound train to see the Ethiopian Emperor, Haile Selassie. He was a short man with a beard, but looked so proud and regal.

Before the Second World War, the Island railways were very busy and there always seemed to be queues of passengers for trains at St John's Road, for in those days nearly every one used the railways. When the race meetings were on at Ashey, Ryde St John's Road was just like Waterloo in the rush hour with race goers, bookies and travelling ticket inspectors and so forth. One day I decided to take my wife and daughter to Ventnor Carnival for a treat. On our return journey we discovered that the Ventnor-Ryde train was packed – every compartment and even the guard's van. The driver therefore invited us up into the cab of his O2 tank. It was just like being in a bakery. What a contrast this scene was to the present day patronage of the Island railways.

After completing my time at St John's Road I had sufficient experience to move on to the Island relief staff. My duties involved looking after various stations, signal boxes, and even guard's rosters while staff were on holiday or off sick. This allowed me access to every line on the Isle of Wight. On one occasion I was sent out on a Sunday to work at Freshwater station. On the Freshwater line trains crossed at Ningwood and the single-line occupation was with a staff on one side of Ningwood and a ticket on the other. Somehow there was a mix up and the train arrived at Freshwater with the wrong single-line safety device. This prevented the Newport train from proceeding any further and it was held at Ningwood. Meanwhile, I was dispatched on my motorcycle with the fireman of the locomotive which had arrived at Freshwater, to Ningwood with the single-line staff.

I eventually settled down to become a signalman at Whippingham where I left the railway in 1953 when the station closed. Whilst working at Whippingham one day, I recall an unusual occurrence when passing a 'down' Cowes bound passenger train hauled by an O2 tank engine, and 'up' Medina Wharf–Ryde freight train hauled by an E1 tank locomotive. I let the freight train in and it stopped, allowing the 'down' passenger train to enter the loop line. After giving the driver of the passenger train the single-line tablet, I wandered back to my signal box to telephone the neighbouring signal box at Haven Street and notify them of how many wagons were in the freight train. Presently, I heard a, "chuff, chuff" and the clatter of wagons. I looked out and to my surprise I saw the E1 heading off past the signal which was set against it and through the points. Not knowing what was going on, I signalled to Haven Street "Vehicles running away!". The result of this unauthorised action was that the points were split and rendered out of action until the permanent way staff could attend to repairs. When the railway authorities heard about this incident an enquiry was held at Woking and this resulted in the freight train driver and fireman being suspended for a few days.

Whippingham station closed in 1953 and I decided to close this chapter in my life and left the railway service.

G. E. 'Ted' Bowers

Most of my railway career was spent in or around Ryde. I started off at Ryde Pier Head in April 1946. Within a few days I was transferred to Ryde St John's Road as Walter Lee had an accident when he fell out of an apple tree at his home in Bembridge, and I therefore had to cover his duties.

Not long after this I was sent back to the Pier Head to work in the Station Master's Office. A preoccupation of railwaymen at this station was fishing in between train arrivals and departures. I for one did not take this up on a regular basis. In fact, I only did fish once and that was on a Good Friday night when I caught three $2\frac{1}{2}$ lb bass. After about two hours I decided to return home only to be confronted by a worried wife who thought I must have been involved in a road accident.

The railway staff were also responsible for the docking of paddle steamers and motor vessels at Ryde Pier Head for the service to and from Portsmouth. One winter's morning when a paddle steamer was departing a railwayman called Fred Budden was easing off a bow rope. Instead of giving out more slack rope Fred decided to hold on, but he could not hold the weight of the PS *Whippingham* and into the drink he went complete with his railway issued greatcoat! His colleague, Jack Corney, had to fish him out. On another occasion Hubert Salter drove a Lister Auto Truck right over the side of Ryde Pier at the end of number three platform. Luckily, Hubert was not seriously injured and the auto truck was recovered from the sea.

Almost everyday I had to travel back and forth between the Pier Head, Esplanade and St John's Road stations on various clerical matters. On one winter's day I set off down the pier behind engine No. 14 *Fishbourne* with Jim Hunnybun at the regulator. With flooding reported in the tunnel Jim set off cautiously into Ryde Tunnel. Not far into the tunnel, I recall the little O2 tank coming to a stop. The flood water was so deep it got into 14's firebox and, as a passenger in the carriages, I could clearly smell the acrid smell of hot sulphurous fumes. Somehow Jim managed to get his steed going but this experience must have frightened the footplate crew who had to remove the locomotive at St John's Road and take it back onto the shed.

Further down the line an amusing incident happened at Wroxall on one occasion that I recall vividly. Porter-Guard Fred Budden, who was mentioned earlier, gave the right away to the driver with his green flag. As the train pulled away he missed climbing aboard but he caught hold of the bar at the very end of the carriage and placed his feet on the buffer! What an unusual way to travel down Apse Bank I thought.

Just at the foot of Apse Bank I used to have an allotment at Shanklin, right next to the main line to Ventnor. Even in my off duty hours there was no

"Happy Dreams"
George Bowers & "Roley" Townsen

escaping my colleagues. I was always on my guard for the passage of engine No. 22 *Brading*. If her driver one, Jack Sturgess, ever spotted me digging away I could be certain of a shower from his peep pipe. Such was the spirit of the Island railways in those days of the steam era.

Owen Attrill

In 1930, I was lucky enough to become a junior parcel porter at St Helens station on the Brading–Bembridge branch. I arrived punctually for my first morning to be greeted by the Station Master, Mr Thomas Clayton Weeks. He was a most unusual character and as often as not he was without collar and tie or arrived at work requiring a shave. He never wore a hat, but was nevertheless an outstanding railwayman. Mr Weeks was actually responsible for St Helens station and the neighbouring St Helens Quay. The Station Master at the neighbouring station of Bembridge was also the Station Master of Brading. Mr May, who looked after these two stations, had a unique position.

SOUTHERN RAILWAY.

LONDON (WEST) OPERATING AND COMMERCIAL DIVISIONS.

HB.

TELEPHONE:
NEWPORT 93.

Office of Assistant for Isle of Wight,

NEWPORT, I. OF W.

REFERENCE.
MY S. 214

YOUR

14th March 1930

Mr Weeks.,
    St Helens.

Dear Sir,

Jr Parcel Porter Owen William Attrill.

Will you please note the appointment of the above named
youth at St Helens is confirmed, and he has received instructions
to report to you on Monday next 17th inst, to commence learning
his duties. His name should be entered on your paybill on and from
that date at 20/- per week, and the enclosed extract from Rules &
Regs handed to him, his signature for same being given on attached
form, which please return to me. Please let me know immediately
you consider him competent to take over his duties, and so
release Jr Pcl Porter Bushell for transfer to Yarmouth.

Yours truly,

For A. S.

About a year after starting at St Helens I recall a Beyer Peacock 2-4-0 tank breaking down before it actually entered Bembridge station. The driver sent his young fireman, who was Walter Buckett the guard's son, to sprint down the track with the single-line key to Brading signal box. A locomotive was then sent up the branch to push the lame duck engine and carriages into Bembridge station.

My work often used to take me down to St Helen's Quay, where up to 13 wharfingers worked unloading the boats. I was amazed to see a row of eight wooden framed and wooden buffered engineers wagons in regular use. On closer inspection I observed that these veteran wagons had their wooden frames extended horizontally at each end of the wagon to form the buffers. About twelve months later, in 1932, they were broken up, but I recall seeing them in use at nights, loaded with ballast which had been dredged up from the harbour entrance, on permanent way relaying and ballasting trains. The year 1932 also saw the departure of my Station Master, Mr Weeks. He was replaced by Mr C. D. Wilcox from Egham. Unfortunately, for our new Station Master he used to compare St Helens with his former station and was often heard to comment on the platform, "When I was at Egham we did ..." The staff and passengers soon cottoned on to this mannerism and he obtained the nickname, 'Egham'.

In the early thirties at St Helens station everyone seemed to know everyone else, and the footplate crews and guards knew their regular passengers extremely well. There was one particular passenger who had difficulty in getting up each morning for the 8.30am train. He would regularly run up the station approach shouting at the top of his voice, "Hold that train". The footplate crews nicknamed this passenger, 'Derby', as he used to run for the train at the speed of a horse. Very rarely was he ever left behind. The driver would often pull his engine's whistle out of devilment to ensure a good gallop up the platform from 'Derby' however!

My position as a junior parcels porter at St Helens came to an end in 1934, and I was transferred to Ryde Pier Head. There I was like others, a bit of a 'Jack of all trades' and besides doing porters' work, we were called upon to do guards' duties, shunting and goods work. On some occasions I drove the Lister Auto Trucks on the pier. The Southern Railway authorities also asked me to drive the pier trams for the Summer Timetables of 1936 and 1937. This was a pretty monotonous job, driving up and down the pier between Ryde Esplanade and Pier Head, loaded with passengers and their luggage. There was one amusing incident that sticks out in my mind from those two summers,

Shunter Frederick Attrill of Ryde Pier Head poses for the camera. Note the unique arm band, 'S.W.&S.C.R.', denoting the fact that Ryde Pier was jointly managed at this time by the LSWR and the LBSCR.

The Attrill Family Collection

who, between them, covered early and late turns of duty. My own box duty was for a three-hour turn mid-day. Sam was a genial character, always whistling at work. Ernest was a quiet character whose interest other than his work was growing roses. His off duty weekends were spent in the country collecting briars on which he would graft the roots and heads of roses to make standards. Sadly, Sam Plumbley died in 1941 and his position in Ryde Pier Head box was filled by George Hallam. During the summer of 1939 I was sent out to Smallbrook Junction for the Summer Timetable but the box was closed earlier than usual in September due to the start of the Second World War. One morning we had a fatality in the Smallbrook section. Trackman Ralph Osborne was walking the permanent way length from Ashey to Ryde when he was knocked down and killed. It's always sad to hear of such an accident on the railways, but when you know the chap it really hurts.

Left, Junior Porter Cedric Attrill and right, Station Master Mr Spinks at Wootton station on 24th November 1931. Mr Spinks was famed for having just one arm, following injury during the First World War, but he was an outstanding railway man who could do any job asked of him.

The Attrill Family Collection

when Driver George Frampton drove the Grapes car tram up over the stop blocks! I don't think the railway authorities were so amused as this particular tram had an interesting historical background. The tram was going to meet the mid-night boat from Portsmouth and luckily was empty, but the accident damaged the carvings located on the corners of the pillars of the Grapes car tram. It was almost written off there and then as there were bits of polished mahogany everywhere, but happily this historical tram survives, fully restored to its original form to this day in Hull Museum.

Being an ambitious man, I applied for a position as a porter-signalman at Ryde Pier Head signal box, to replace Horace Tubbs who, after a spell in this position, was returning to the mainland from where he originated. My application was successful and I joined Ernest Shepherd and Sam Plumbley

SOUTHERN RAILWAY.

(⁴⁰⁄₅₉) Ryde Pier Signalbox Thursday 29th day of December 1938

DESCRIPTION OF TRAIN	REAR SECTION					Train Arrived		Train Departed		ADVANCE SECTION					REMARKS.
	Time described	Is Line Clear Received	Is Line Clear Accepted	Train entering Section Received	Train out of Section Sent	Line on	Actual Time	Line on	Actual Time	Time described	Is Line Clear Sent	Is Line Clear Accepted	Train entering Section Sent	Train out of Section Received	
B 4.0								4	4.14	4.9	4.9	4.14	4.26		
dl 4.5								3	4.16	4.20	4.20	4.20	4.29		
B 7.0								2	7.0	6.58	6.58	7.0	7.12		
dl 7.5								4	7.5	7.12	7.12	7.12	7.16		
" 7.45								3	7.45	7.41	7.41	7.45	7.59		
" 6.5	7 & P							1	8.0	7.59	7.59	8.0	8.20		
B 8.25								2	8.25	8.23	8.23	8.25	8.33		
dl 8.35								3	8.35	8.33	8.33	8.35	8.44		
" 9.25								1	9.27	9.23	9.23	9.27	9.37		
B 9.35								2	9.37	9.37	9.37	9.37	9.46		
dl Eng								1	9.54	9.44	9.44	9.54	9.58		
" 10.28								1	10.25	10.24	10.24	10.25	10.35		
B 10.35								2	10.35	10.35	10.35	10.35	10.43		
dl 11.28								1	11.25	11.22	11.22	11.25	11.36		
B 11.35								2	11.35	11.36	11.36	11.36	11.44		
dl 12.28								1	12.25	12.23	12.23	12.25	12.34		
B 12.35								2	12.35	12.34	12.34	12.34	12.44		
M 1.28								1	1.25	1.22	1.22	1.25	1.34		
B 1.35								2	1.35	1.34	1.34	1.35	1.42		
M 2.28								1	2.24	2.26	2.26	2.24	2.36		
B 2.35								2	2.35	2.36	2.36	2.36	2.43		
M 3.28								1	3.26	3.22	3.22	3.26	3.33		
B 3.35								2	3.35	3.35	3.35	3.35	3.43		
M 4.28								1	4.25	4.34	4.34	4.35	4.34		
B 4.35								3	4.35	4.34	4.34	4.35	4.43		
M 5.28								4	5.26	5.23	5.23	5.26	5.35		
B 5.35								3	5.35	5.35	5.35	5.35	5.44		
M 6.28								4	6.24	6.24	6.24	6.24	6.38		
B 6.35								3	6.35	6.38	6.38	6.38	6.43		
M 7.28								4	7.30	7.30	7.30	7.30	7.38		
B 7.35								3	7.36	7.38	7.38	7.38	7.43		
M 8.28								1	8.25	8.22	8.22	8.25	8.34		
B 8.35								2	8.35	8.34	8.34	8.35	8.43		
M Engine 8.40								4	8.57	8.43	8.43	8.47	8.51		
M Engine 9.5								1	9.23	9.18	9.18	9.23	9.27		
M 9.40								1	9.40	9.40	9.40	9.41	9.49		
B 9.45								2	9.45	9.45	9.45	9.45	9.53		

Closed to St Johns. 9.54 p.

TRAIN REGISTER BOOK.
UP TRAINS.

Ryde Pier Signalbox Thursday 29th day of December 193 2 (Stock 985 11/32)

DESCRIPTION OF TRAIN	REAR SECTION					Train Arrived		Train Departed		ADVANCE SECTION					REMARKS.
	Time described	Is Line Clear Received	Is Line Clear Accepted	Train entering Section Received	Train out of Section Sent	Line on	Actual Time	Line on	Actual Time	Time described	Is Line Clear Sent	Is Line Clear Accepted	Train entering Section Sent	Train out of Section Received	
M Goods	3.0	3.0	3.5	3.12	3										E Shepherd on duty 3.0 A.M.
B Emp	3.26	3.26	3.29	3.31	2										Opened to St John's Rd 3.0"
M Empty	6.11	6.11	6.16	6.20	3										
B 6.42	6.25	6.25	6.37	6.42	2										
M 7.15	7.3	7.3	7.10	7.15	3										
" Emp	7.41	7.41	7.42	7.49	1										
" Empty	7.49	7.49	7.53	7.58	3										
B 8.11	7.56	7.58	8.6	8.11	2										
M 8.22	8.11	8.11	8.18	8.23	3										
B 9.18	9.6	9.6	9.13	9.18	2										
M 9.22	9.18	9.18	9.18	9.23	4										
" Emp	9.56	9.59	10.1	10.4	1										
B 10.13	10.8	10.4	10.7	10.13	2										
M 10.22	10.12	10.12	10.19	10.24	3										
B 11.12	10.53	10.58	11.5	11.10	2										
M 11.22	11.10	11.10	11.16	11.23	3										
B 12.12	11.58	11.58	12.5	12.12	2										
M 12.22	12.12	12.12	12.16	12.22	3										E Shepherd off duty 12.30 P.M.
B 1.12	12.55	12.55	1.5	1.11	2										W Attrill on duty 12.30 p.m.
M 1.22	1.11	1.11	1.14	1.22	3										
B 2.12	1.56	1.56	2.5	2.11	2										
M 2.22	2.11	2.11	2.14	2.22	3										
B 3.12	2.56	2.56	3.6	3.11	2										
M 3.22	3.11	3.11	3.17	3.22	3										
B 4.12	3.57	3.57	4.6	4.11	2										
M 4.22	4.11	4.11	4.14	4.22	3										
M Goods	Regs	4.50	4.50	4.50				Cancelled 4.56p.							
B 5.12	4.56	4.565	5.4	5.11	3										
M 5.22	5.11	5.11	5.18	5.23	2										
M Goods	Regs	5.54	5.54	5.54				Cancelled 6.2p.							
B 6.12	6.2	6.2	6.10	6.4	3										
M 6.22	6.4	6.4	6.18	6.24	2										
B 7.12	6.56	6.56	7.6	7.11	3										
M 7.22	7.11	7.11	7.18	7.22	2										
B 8.12	7.55	7.55	8.5	8.10	2										
M 8.22	8.10	8.10	8.16	8.22	3										
M Ktie.	8.51	8.51	8.58	9.2	3										
M 9.23	9.12	9.12	9.18	9.23	3										
B 9.28	9.23	9.23	9.23	9.31	2										
			Reg W Attrill off duty 10.0pm.												

Owen Attrill pictured at St Helen's station in September 1934 with a lady passenger.

The Attrill Family Collection

Owing to the premature closure of Smallbrook box in 1939, I transferred back to regular duties at Ryde Pier box. My family had long associations with the railway on Ryde Pier as my father, Frederick William Attrill, started work in 1910 as a porter for the London & South Western Railway/London, Brighton & South Coast Railway Joint Company, which administered the pier. Like me, my father was promoted to porter signalman and worked in the Pier Head box. On odd occasions he also worked in the old signal boxes at Ryde Esplanade and Ryde St John's Road North. He didn't like this job and soon became a shunter, but when the Southern Railway took over in 1923 this particular job was downgraded. One thing I will always treasure is the memory of working with my dad on the railways in those days, which must have been quite unusual – especially as we both worked at the same station!

My father was a bit of a joker I discovered. I will always remember the time when Mr French, the Station Master retired. My father decided to use this situation to play a practical joke on his good friend and colleague Sid Sartin, who was a porter

at Ryde Pier Head. Sid always liked to sing and fancied himself as an aspiring professional. My father therefore informed Sid that he was invited to sing at the Station Master's retirement party. Of course this was not true, but Sid took the proposition seriously and turned up at Mr French's house ready and prepared. Meanwhile, my father and his co-conspirator Harry Driver, followed Sid up to the Station Master's house to look on. They hid themselves in the garage of a doctor's house opposite, but their behaviour attracted the attention of the doctor's daughter. She in turn contacted the local police who took the two suspects back to the police station for questioning. They both explained that it was all a practical joke within the Isle of Wight railway community. The police therefore decided to release my father and his colleague Harry, but unfortunately a local reporter was on hand and the whole incident was reported in the newspaper. This time, at least, Sid Sartin had the last laugh on his mates!

This photograph was taken on 5th May 1934 at Ryde Pier and shows left to right, Jim Attrill (tram conductor), Bill Buckingham and Harry Saville (both Borough of Ryde ticket collectors).

The Attrill Family Collection

My father worked at Ryde Pier Head until he died at the age of 51 years in 1937. For a few years the Attrill Family dominated the railway scene, in numbers that is. My younger brother Jim started on the Island railways and by coincidence joined the service on the same day as myself, 17th March 1930. Young Jim however joined my father at Ryde Pier, but he worked on the trams with Driver Reg Aylward. He used to enjoy going up and down all day collecting ¾d fares. After a few years he was promoted to Ryde St John's Road as a porter and later became leading porter, which involved some shunting in St John's yard. The fourth member of the family to work on the Island

This picture was taken at Ryde Pier Head during the 1930s. Left, W. Shockridge (station foreman), centre, Frederick Attrill (shunter) and right, George Blackman (ticket collector).
The Attrill Family Collection

With a full head of steam and Westinghouse brake pump panting furiously, No. 16 *Ventnor* sets off from Ryde St John's Road station with a train for Newport and Cowes.
G. M. Kichenside

SMALLBROOK JUNCTION SIGNAL BOX

Smallbrook Junction signal box was demolished and burned on the site in the late 1960s.

A summer Saturday Ryde–Ventnor fast train is brought to a halt at Smallbrook Junction inner-home signal by Signalman Vic Hailes.
J. R. G. Griffiths

railways was my older brother, Cedric, who started in Ryde Works in 1928. He later went on to work at Wootton station, where he was opposite turn of duty to Mr Spinks, the one-armed Station Master. Mr Spinks was a military man and persuaded my older brother to join the Royal Corp of Signals. However, after finishing his time in the Army, Cedric returned to work on the Island railways at St John's and later Haven Street. The final family connection with the Island railways was my father-in-law, Frederick Lynton, who was a guard dating back to the days of the Isle of Wight Central Railway. He lived next to Driver Cecil 'Bill' Miller at Wootton, but sadly passed away at the early age of just 34.

At the outbreak of the Second World War in 1939, several Island railwaymen volunteered to join one of the armed services. Unfortunately, by working on the railways we were termed a 'reserved occupation'. Many of us didn't give up there however, and I for one applied to join His Majesty's Forces but being a porter-signalman my application for release was once again rejected. Not long afterwards the Civil Defence Volunteers (CDV) were formed, later becoming the Local Defence Volunteers (LDV) and then the Home Guard. The Isle of Wight Railway Section of the Home Guard was formed on 15th July 1940 and I soon joined up.

We were part of the 4th Battalion Hampshire Regiment – Home Guards and we were supplied with a special arm-band which we wore on our uniform. The Railway Section of the Home Guard was under orders from the Military at Parkhurst Barracks, where on occasions we underwent training in: drill, bayonet practice, map reading, use of small arms and machine gunnery. After the fall of France in 1940, we really felt that on the Isle of Wight we were in the front line of Britain's defence. The Luftwaffe then started to drop magnetic mines off Ryde Pier Head during their raids. These were deadly devices which were deliberately dropped in the shipping lanes to cause losses of shipping from Portsmouth and Southampton. Our Railway Home Guard was therefore detailed to do nightly observation duties from a small hut at the extreme end of Ryde Pier Head. Inside this hut was installed a horizontal compass with a hand operated spear. Others of these devices were installed at strategic positions on the mainland at five mile intervals. Our assignment was to use these compasses to observe where mines were dropped during air raids. We spotted the parachute mines in the searchlights and took a reading of the location of the drop. This information, with estimated height and time seen would then be dispatched to HMS

A beautiful portrait photograph for the signal enthusiast showing the original lattice post lower quadrant inner-home signal gantry at Smallbrook Junction, complete with metal finials. The left hand arm signal controls the main line ahead to Ventnor and the right hand arm signal controls the line veering off to the right towards Ashey and Havenstreet. The white shirt of Signalman Vic Hailes stands out against the backcloth of woodland scenery.

J. R. G. Griffiths

Medina. We would then watch the Royal Navy mine sweepers promptly head out to deal with the mines. In addition to this we had parades and training at Ryde St John's Road station on Wednesday nights and in St John's Parish Hall on Friday nights.

For the record, as I doubt if this has ever been recorded before, the Home Guard Railway Section Company Commander was Mr P. Harding, who was normally based in the Southern Railway Advertising Section. The Home Guard officer in charge at Ryde Pier Head was Charlie Reeves who could normally be found as a booking clerk.

Vic Hailes

Geoffrey M. Kichenside, the former editor of *Railway World* once wrote in that periodical that I was the most photographed railwayman anywhere on the British Railways' network. This statement could well have been true as when I was signalman at Smallbrook Junction signal box there were always railway enthusiasts snapping pictures from the lineside or, when passing on trains. However, my railway career on the Island began elsewhere.

My brother Ron was a signalman and I always wanted to follow in his footsteps and join him as a signalman on the railways. When a post became vacant at Newchurch on the Sandown–Newport line, my brother put in a good word for me and I started. That's how it was in those days, the Island railways were a 'family affair'.

Newchurch was quite a busy little place in those days as Island residents mainly relied on the railway for shopping and general business. The platform was on the south side of the line with the station building standing adjacent to the level crossing. Newchurch station was roughly two miles from Sandown, but was half-a-mile north of the actual village it served. There was good holiday traffic through the summer season, and this was followed by the sugar beet season. The beet was grown in the Arreton Valley and sent to Selby in Yorkshire, via our single long siding. This siding

Left: **Junior Porter Vic Hailes aged 15 years at Newchurch station in 1936. In later life he went on to work at Smallbrook Junction signal box where without doubt, he became the most photographed employee on British Railways.**

J. R. G. Griffiths

Opposite page: **Smallbrook Junction signal box – possibly the most photographed signal box on British Railways.**

J. R. G. Griffiths

was controlled by the train staff and ticket, which opened the small ground frame. We also had a lot of work each night in loading up consigments of locally grown flowers, which were dispatched to Covent Garden in London. A special four-wheel PMV utility van would be attached to a Newport–Merstone–Sandown train in the late afternoon for collection of the flowers from Horringford and Newchurch. This van would then proceed to Sandown and be attached to a Ventnor–Ryde train. I stayed at Newchurch for three years until 1938, as a junior porter.

From 1938, I was promoted to become a junior parcel porter at St Helens Quay, which was situated between Brading and Bembridge. People wrongly assume that the majority of freight traffic went through Medina Wharf just outside Cowes. It is true to say that most of the coal traffic went through Medina Wharf, but all the Island stores came into St Helens in those days, including the tar from the South Western distilleries at Southampton. The tar would be transported to Sandown, Shanklin and Ryde. At St Helens Quay we had a weighbridge and two cranes, one of which was hand-operated and one mobile crane which had its own crane road.

Entry to St Helens Quay was under the control of St Helens signal box and No. 3 lever unlocked the level crossing gates. After the passenger service had finished each day, a locomotive would shunt Bembridge station sidings and then come into the quay to shunt and collect full wagons and vans. The goods guard was provided with a shunting list which involved up to 20 different movements each night; up to an hour's work each time. Furthermore, there would be a further hour's work of shunting at St Helens Quay before the passenger service began each morning. Each siding in the quay was given a name – Gas House, Mill Road, Weighbridge Road, Number Four Road, Tarpot Road, Ballaster's Berth Road, Straight Road, Crane Road, Carrier Road, Engine Road, and Airport Road. At one time there was even a narrow gauge track of 1ft 11½in gauge which conveyed coal and coke to the gasworks from the quayside. The Ballaster's Birth Road was reserved for unloading a little barge called, *The Ballaster*, which in my time at St Helens was employed exclusively on dredging the narrow harbour entrance. We would have a rake of six old LBSCR wooden wagons waiting in Ballaster's Birth ready for the silt dredged up. We received locomotive boilers and spares for Ryde

Whilst waiting for the section to clear, Vic Hailes comes out on to the signal box veranda. To his right, E1 class 0-6-0T No. 4 *Wroxall* simmers gently.

J. R. G. Griffiths

Works quite frequently from East leigh Works at Southampton. These locomotive parts were usually brought across the Solent on one of the two barges provided, either the *Bankwell* or the *Hythe*.

Sadly, after the Bembridge branch closed St Helens Quay became synonymous as a dumping ground for withdrawn rolling stock. During the War II was 'called up' to join the Royal Engineers at Longmoor and I didn't return to the Isle of Wight railways until 1946. Initially, I was a porter at Ryde Pier Head, but quickly transferred to Brading as a porter-signalman. It was during this period, in the summer of 1947, that I was first called to work at Smallbrook Junction signal box and from then on I went there to work each summer. During the winter of 1948 I transferred back to Ryde Pier as signalman in the Pier box.

In the early days at Smallbrook Junction only one photographer came out to photograph me at work and that was none other than Joe Griffiths. It wasn't until towards the end of steam, from about 1958 onwards, that Smallbrook began to be photographed regularly. It was the busiest single-line signal box on British Railways and quite often I would have three different trains under my control. Although it was only a small, 20-lever ground frame, it governed the smooth operation of the train service during the summer months. It was originally opened by the Southern Railway back in 1926 and remained unaltered until it was closed on

17th September 1966. As the signal box at Smallbrook was so remote, there was no mains electricity and no running water. In fact, the only access to the box was via the railway.

The interesting thing about Smallbrook Junction signal box was that it was only open during the summer months, from May until September. During the winter season the points were clipped and the signal arms removed and placed inside the signal box. The running sections of line then operated as two independent lines: Ryde St John's Road to Haven Street and Ryde St John's Road to Brading. On hot days the box used to get like an oven and I prayed for the sun to go down on many occasions. One never had time to sit outside, with twelve trains an hour on peak summer Saturdays. For most of the day there was always a train somewhere on the blocks and there was barely enough time to go to the toilet!

There was only one instance during which I experienced a major problem at Smallbrook and this was when a single line token on the Smallbrook–Brading section went missing. Strangely enough, it involved the now preserved No. 24 *Calbourne*. I remember making the token exchange at the time with the crew of the passing train which

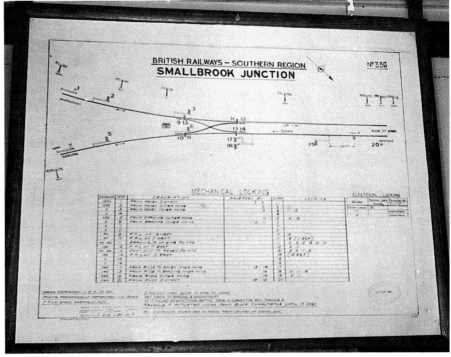

The reason for the delay becomes apparent, as Signalman Vic Hailes collects the single line token from the driver of No. 22 *Brading*, which passes by light engine heading towards Ryde. No. 4 *Wroxall* pauses at Smallbrook with heavy freight train of coal from Medina Wharf.

J. R. G. Griffiths

Inside Smallbrook signal box; the framed track diagram.

Dr John Mackett

was bound for Ventnor. Some minutes later Signalman Roy Way 'phoned from Brading to inform me that the single-line token pouch did not contain a key token! This completely baffled me and I asked that *Calbourne*'s crew check in their cab to ascertain that the token had not fallen out. Driver Ken West and Fireman Joe Maxfield searched their footplate in vain. Meanwhile, a piloting arrangement had to be brought into use between Brading and Smallbrook until the token machine could be balanced. I believe that they even took engine 24 out of service on the 'up' run and returned her to St John's Road depot, where her fire was dropped and the ashes raked through to double check for the

DOWN TRAINS

BRITISH RAILWAYS

Smallbrook Jct Signalbox — Satur day 4 day of July 1964

DESCRIPTION OF TRAIN	REAR SECTION					Train Arrived		Train Departed		ADVANCE SECTION					REMARKS
	Time described	Is Line Clear Received	Is Line Clear Accepted	Train entering Section Received	Train out of Section Sent	Line on	Actual Time	Line on	Actual Time	Time described	Is Line Clear Sent	Is Line Clear Accepted	Train entering Section Sent	Train out of Section Received	
On duty 3.55am Davies															
4 o c.	4.7	11	16							4.11	13	20			
4.5 V	4.14	19	21							4.19	21	28			
Eng &Bn	5.43	43	47							5.44	47	54			
6.16 V	6.43	47	50							6.47	50	56			
6.55 V	6.56	7.10	13							7.10	13	23			
7.7 c	7.13	15	18							7.15	18	28			
7.40 V	7.40	48	51							7.48	50	56			
2 of cls V	7.56	8.4	19	7	18.					8.18	19	26			
8.25 c	8.25	39	42							8.39	42	51			
8.35 V	8.42	45	48							8.45	48	55			
Eng. Sk.	8.57	9.1	3							9.1	3	8.			
9.25 V	9.28	36	39							9.36	39	45			
9.30 c	9.39	41	45							9.41	45	54			
E C S o/Bn	9.41	002	07							10.04	06	13			
10.05 V	10.07	14	20			17.				10.18	19	26			
10.25 V	10.34	41	44							10.41	44	51			
10.30 c	10.44	46	49							10.46	49	57			
11.05 V	11.11	17	27	20	26.					11.25	26	33			
11.25 V	11.33	39	44	Outer						11.47	44	50			
11.30 c	11.44	45	47							11.45	47				Advised 1720 that
S/Bcl Sk	11.53	56	58							11.53	58	12.04			1130 c. disabled
12.05 V	12.15	22	25							12.22	25	31			at Ashey.
12.25 V	12.38	45	48							12.45	48	54			Asst. Eng &B 11.53
13.05 c V	13.09	15	26	19	26					13.25	26	33			12.31 to protel
Off duty 13.30 hrs Davies							RR Drake on duty 13.30 hrs								to S J Rd.
13.05 V	13.34	40	48	43	46					13.41	46	53			An. 13.00 hrs.
Eng 45 in	13.48	48	51							1.48	51	3.0			Cancelled to Ashey
S/Bcl V	13.51	53	57							1.53	57	14.3			13.00 hrs.
14.5 V	14.10	14	18							14.14	17	23			
14.25 V	14.24	35	44	39						14.43	43	50			
15.5 V	15.5	12	24	17						15.22	23	30			
Q S/Bcl Sk	15.26	28	32							15.30	32	38			
15.25 V	15.32	51	53							15.51	53	59			
15.30 c	16.8	14	17							16.14	17	25			
Q S/Bcl Sk	15.59	16.3	.5							16.3	.5	11			
16.5 V	16.17	20	23							16.20	23	28			
16.25 V	16.37	45	51							16.49	50	56			
17.5 V	17.11	17	21							17.17	21	27			
17.25 V	17.31	34	40							17.38	40	46			
17.30 c	17.55	60	.3							18.0	.3	17			
18.5 V	18.7	14	18							18.17	18	25			
18.25 V	18.28	36	39							18.36	39	44			
18.30 c	18.39	40	43							18.40	43	54			
19.25 V	19.33	38	42							19.38	42	50			
19.30 c	19.42	45	54							19.45	48	56			
20.25 V	20.26	35	38							20.35	38	45			
20.30 c	20.38	39	41							20.39	41	51			
21.35 c	21.37	44	47							21.44	47	55			
21.40 V	21.47	49	54							21.49	54	57			
22.15 V	22.14	23	25							22.23	25	31			
Closing Haven St 22.05 hrs															
Bcg 22.25 hrs															
St Rd 22.30 hrs															
R R Drake off duty															

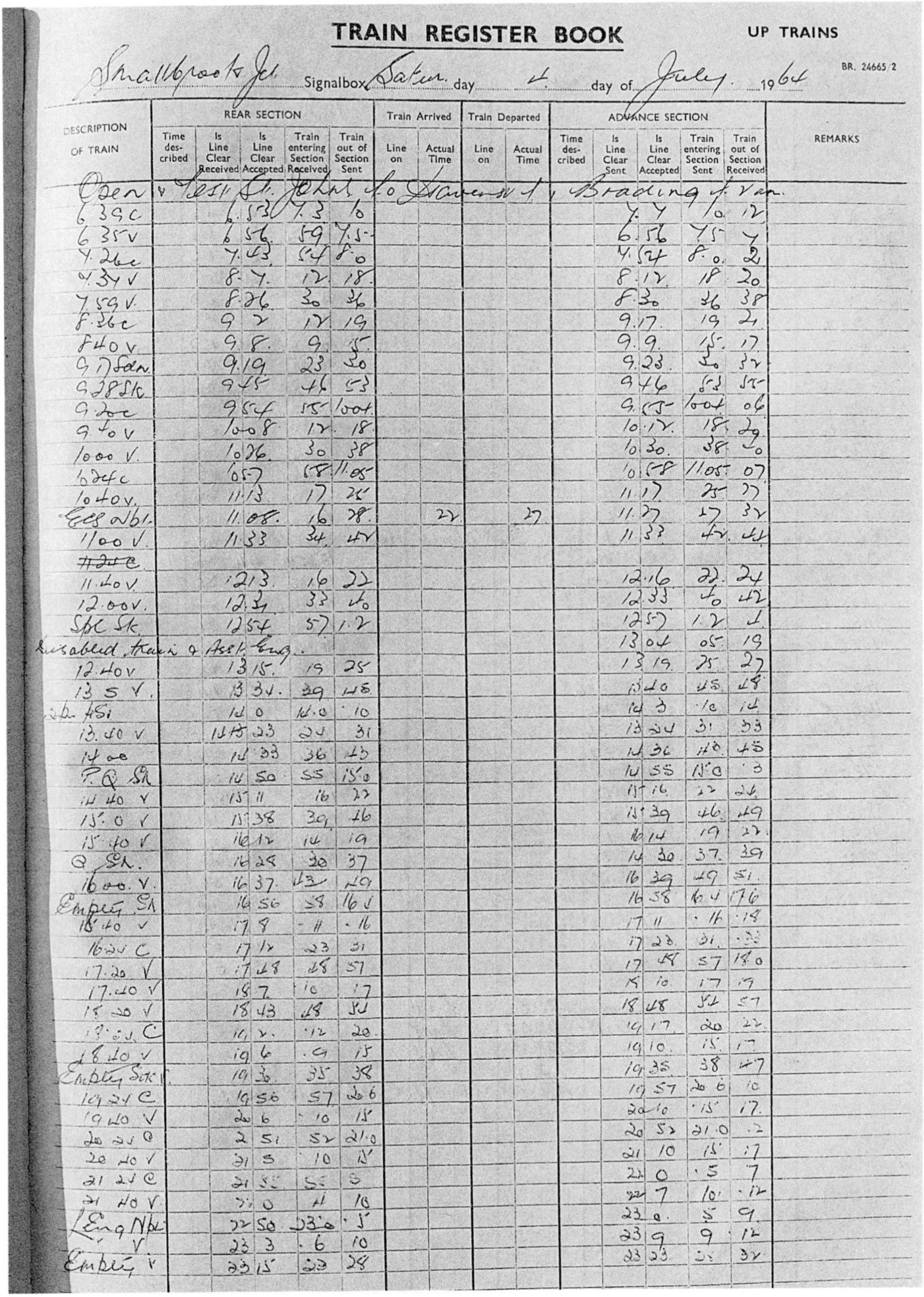

TRAIN REGISTER BOOK

UP TRAINS

BR. 24665/2

Smallbrook Jc. Signalbox Satur. day 4 day of July 1964

DESCRIPTION OF TRAIN	REAR SECTION: Time described	REAR SECTION: Is Line Clear Received	REAR SECTION: Is Line Clear Accepted	REAR SECTION: Train entering Section Received	REAR SECTION: Train out of Section Sent	Train Arrived: Line on	Train Arrived: Actual Time	Train Departed: Line on	Train Departed: Actual Time	ADVANCE SECTION: Time described	ADVANCE SECTION: Is Line Clear Sent	ADVANCE SECTION: Is Line Clear Accepted	ADVANCE SECTION: Train entering Section Sent	ADVANCE SECTION: Train out of Section Received	REMARKS
Open & Test St. Johns to Haven st. & Brading & Van.															
6.39C		6.53		7.3	10						7.4		10	12	
6.35V		6.56		59	7.5						6.56		7.5	7	
7.26C		7.43		54	8.0						7.54		8.0	2	
7.34V		8.7		12	18						8.12		18	20	
7.59V		8.26		30	36						8.30		36	38	
8.36C		9.2		12	19						9.17		19	21	
8.40V		9.8		9	15						9.9		15	17	
9.17 San.		9.19		23	30						9.23		30	32	
9.28 Sk.		9.45		46	53						9.46		53	55	
9.20C		9.54		55	10.04						9.55		10.04	06	
9.40V		10.08		12	18						10.12		18	29	
10.00V		10.26		30	38						10.30		38	40	
10.24C		10.57		58	11.05						10.58		11.05	07	
10.40V		11.13		17	25						11.17		25	27	
Ecs Nbl.		11.08		16	28		22		27		11.27		27	32	
11.00V		11.33		34	42						11.33		42	44	
~~11.24C~~															
11.40V		12.13		16	22						12.16		22	24	
12.00V		12.34		33	40						12.33		40	42	
Spl Sk.		12.54		57	1.2						12.57		1.2	4	
Disabled train & Asst. Eng.											13.04		05	19	
12.40V		13.15		19	25						13.19		25	27	
13.5V		13.34		39	48						13.40		45	48	
2 Pn. ASi		14.0		14.0	10						14.3		10	14	
13.40V		14.15 23		24	31						13.24		31	33	
14.00		14.33		36	43						14.36		40	45	
P.Q. Sh.		14.50		55	15.0						14.55		15.0	3	
14.40V		15.11		16	22						15.16		22	24	
15.0V		15.38		39	46						15.39		46	49	
15.40V		16.12		14	19						16.14		19	22	
Q. Sh.		16.28		30	37						16.30		37	39	
16.00V		16.37		43	49						16.39		49	51	
Empty Sh.		16.56		58	16.4						16.58		16.4	17.6	
16.40V		17.8		11	16						17.11		16	18	
16.24C		17.12		23	31						17.23		31	33	
17.20V		17.48		48	57						17.48		57	18.0	
17.40V		18.7		10	17						18.10		17	19	
18.20V		18.43		48	54						18.48		54	57	
18.24C		19.2		12	20						19.17		20	22	
18.40V		19.6		9	15						19.10		15	17	
Empty Stk.		19.30		35	38						19.35		38	47	
19.24C		19.56		57	20.6						19.57		20.6	10	
19.40V		20.6		10	15						20.10		15	17	
20.24C		20.51		52	21.0						20.52		21.0	2	
20.40V		21.5		10	15						21.10		15	17	
21.24C		21.55		55	3						22.0		5	7	
21.40V		22.0		4	10						22.7		10	12	
L Eng Nbl.		22.50		23.0	5						23.0		5	9	
V		23.3		6	10						23.9		9	12	
Empty V		23.15		23	28						23.23		30	32	

The pictures show the Train Register Book for Smallbrook Junction for Saturday 4th July 1964. The entries by Vic Hailes and Ray Draper are of particular interest as they note that the 11.30am Cowes train is propelled from Ashey to Ryde St John's Road, passing Smallbrook at 13.00hrs.

R. J. Blenkinsop

Signalman Vic Hailes
at work inside Small-
brook Junction signal
box.

G. M. Kichenside

missing token. Along with Cyril Henley I checked the box and surrounding vegetation for that token but all to no avail. Quite what happened to it I will never know and the mystery remains unresolved to this day. If it is ever found in the future I would love to know. My colleagues have never forgotten that incident and occasionally I will get a bit of leg pull about a token tree that has been spotted growing out on the site of Smallbrook box!

On another occasion at Smallbrook Junction I pulled levers 20, 19 and 17 to allow a Ryde–Newport train to pass. Normally it would only take two or three minutes for a train to cover this section, but after ten minutes I became suspicious as to its whereabouts. Eventually I observed an approaching fireman. He informed me that the outer-home signal was 'off'. "I know," I replied, "that's how it should be". However, the fireman pointed out to me that the whole red signal arm of the upper quadrant signal was laying on the

ground! A flagman was then sent for to allow trains to pass until Cyril Henley repaired the arm.

One afternoon out at Smallbrook box I recall having a temporary bell failure when everything went silent. After about ten minutes things mysteriously returned to normal. What ever was the reason for this? About half-an-hour later the lengthman, Bill Dyer, called into the box. "Did you have anything go wrong in the box?" he enquired. I repeated what had happened to Bill. He then informed me that he had cut through the wires whilst lopping down some branches of a tree. Luckily, in Bill's pocket was a rabbit wire, so he used this to make a running repair. This was a piece of pure Isle of Wight railway improvisation that was commonplace in those days!

Just before 2pm one summer afternoon I signed on duty at Smallbrook and relieved Ray Draper. The weather had been very hot and thousands of tourists had swarmed onto the Island beaches. It

BRITISH RAILWAYS (S)
Railway Correspondence & Travel Society.
Available on Day of issue only
Circular Rail Tour of
ISLE OF WIGHT
from Ryde P.H. via
NEWPORT, COWES, FRESHWATER
VENTNOR WEST, MERSTONE
SANDOWN, BRADING & BEMBRIDGE
and BACK. 18th MAY 1952
THIRD CLASS
NOT TRANSFERABLE
0504   0504

2nd - PRIVILEGE   PRIVILEGE - 2nd
SINGLE   SINGLE
0563   Brading to   0563
Brading   Brading
Sandown   Sandown
SANDOWN
(S)   2d. Fare 2d.   (S)
For conditions see over   For conditions see over

2nd- PRIVILEGE   PRIVILEGE -2nd
RETURN   RETURN
2491   Ventnor   Brading   2491
TO   TO
BRADING   VENTNOR
(S) Fare 10d.   Fare 10d. (S)
For conditions see over   For conditions see over

SOUTHERN RAILWAY.
BRADING HARBOUR EMBANKMENT
ROAD & WORKS
1d   Receipt for one of the
Penny Tolls
enumerated in the author-
ised List exhibited upon the
Bridge premises.
FOR CONDITIONS SEE BACK
L 3969

SOUTHERN RAILWAY.
Issued subject to the Bye-laws, Regulations &
Conditions in the Company's Bills and Notices.
0942   Brading to   0942
SANDOWN
via
First Class. Fare 9d
NOT TRANSFERABLE.

2nd - SINGLE   SINGLE - 2nd
Brading To
2300   Brading   Brading   2300
Ryde St.J.Road   Ryde St.J.Road
RYDE ST. JOHNS ROAD
(S)   8d. FARE 8d.   (S)
For conditions see over   For conditions see over

1787
SOUTHERN RLY
DAY EXCURSION
Available as advertised
BRADING
TO
BEMBRIDGE
THIRD CLASS
FOR CONDITIONS
SEE BACK

A knee-level view of the Smallbrook Junction lever frame.

J. R. G. Griffiths

53

Two photographs of a heavily loaded six-coach train for Ventnor, hauled by No. 14 *Fishbourne* passes Smallbrook Junction with Driver 'Ginger' Minter at the regulator. The photographs were taken from the top of the Cowes line inner home signal – with the permission of Mr G. H. Gardener, Assistant for the Isle of Wight, who was in the signal box.

G. M. Kichenside

No. 26 *Whitwell* ambles into Brading on 19th June 1965, with a six-coach train for Ventnor.   *Tony Scarsbrook*

No. 28 *Ashey* sweeps around the curve into Brading with a train for Ventnor. Note the tall 'up' starting signal with repeater arm lower down the post and the two loaded coal wagons in the small goods yard.

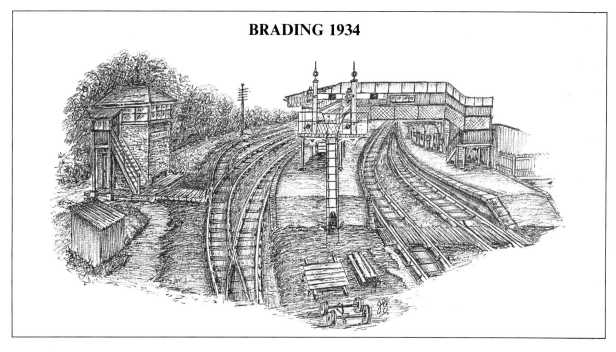

BRADING 1934

Passengers changed here for St Helens and Bembridge.

wasn't long before my first train approached the box, the 2.10pm from Ryde Pier hauled by engine No. 17 *Seaview* with Driver Bill Vallender at the regulator. As the locomotive approached the inner-home signal it halted. Bill climbed down off his engine and walked along to the box and informed me that there was a buckle in the line. The train had

Brading station in its heyday. Points to note for the railway modeller are the delightful posters, the gas lamp on the right and the tall 'up' starting signal beyond the covered footbridge.

J. R. G. Griffiths

to reverse back to St John's Road and single line working was introduced on the 'up' line. Meanwhile, Ganger Charlie French organised the P.W. staff to repair the line where it had expanded. It was a close thing to a near derailment.

When I worked at Brading signal box I used to like to look back through the train register to see if there had been any problems earlier on the previous shift. To my surprise, I read one day that a token had been, quote, "lost in the sand"! On making further enquiries I discovered that some

drivers used to throw the single line hoop into the sand bunker located at the Ryde end of the 'down' platform. The speed of the approaching train had forced the token to become buried in this sand supply, but it was found eventually.

I mentioned earlier that I had a token lost at Smallbrook which was never found. On another occasion, late at night in pitch black darkness, a token was lost and found. I was waiting outside the box to receive the single-line token from a train approaching from Brading. This engine was barking crisply in the darkness and as she approached sparks could be seen shooting out of the chimney like larva from a volcano. Not wishing to have my fingers broken in the token exchange I stood back

as the train roared past at something like forty miles an hour! It was that old rogue Driver Jack Sturgess on his beloved engine No. 22 *Brading*. Well he let go of the hoop and away it bounced into the long grass. It took me some time to find it, but with the use of an oil lamp it was uncovered. In daylight hours Jack's approach to Smallbrook was completely the opposite. He would coast through on 22 *Brading* and then turn the blower full on so that the engine produced clouds of dirty smoke and cinders which would cascade down onto my clean white shirt. Driver Sturgess was someone who used to come to work and enjoy every minute of it! That's how I like to remember those days – fun, friends but hard work – what a memory!

No. 24 *Calbourne* pulls into Brading with an 'up' train from Ventnor on 7th September 1963. It is more than likely that either Ken West or Tony Tiltman are at the controls of their regular engine.

G. M. Kichenside

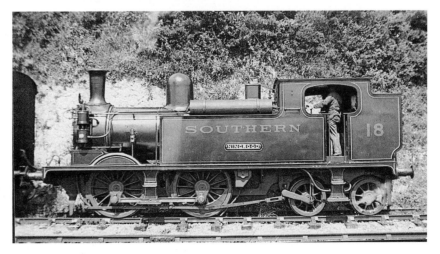

A side view close up of No. 18 *Ningwood* waiting in the Brading Chalk Siding at the head of an empty coach stock working.

The Peter Joyce Collection

SANDOWN

2nd · SINGLE   SINGLE · 2nd
Shanklin to
Shanklin   Shanklin
Sandown   Sandown
SANDOWN
(S) 5d. FARE 5d. (S)
For conditions see over For conditions see over
1385

SOUTHERN RAILWAY,
WEEKLY SEASON TICKET.
No 2824   **7**   **THIRD CLASS**
Available from
Until   **10 SEP 33**
Between
W
SANDOWN
AND ALL STATIONS IN THE
ISLE OF WIGHT
ISSUED SUBJECT TO CONDITIONS ON OTHER SIDE. Rate 7s. 6d.

S. & I. of W. S. P. Co. Ltd. &
BRITISH RYS (S'thern Region)
SOUTHAMPTON to
SANDOWN
Via Cowes, Newport and
Ryde. St. John's Road.
Connection between Boat
and Train not guaranteed
3rd Class Fare 13/-
Including ALL Pier Tolls
0390

BRITISH RAILWAYS (S)
This ticket is issued subject to the Bye-laws,
Regulations and Conditions contained in the
Publications and Notices of and applicable to the
Railway Executive.
Shanklin to
RYDE ESPLANADE or
RYDE ST. JOHN'S ROAD
Via Brading
THIRD CLASS   THIRD CLASS
Fare.1/2 H   Fare 1/2 H
NOT TRANSFERABLE.
8336

Southern Railway.
(3/24) TO Stock 787 G
SANDOWN
Via Portsmouth.

S. & I. of W. S. P. Co. Ltd. &
BRITISH RYS (S'thern Region)
SOUTHAMPTON to
SHANKLIN
Via Cowes, Newport and
Ryde. St. John's Road.
Connection between Boat
and Train not guaranteed
3rd Class Fare 13/9
Including ALL Pier Tolls
0300

SOUTHERN RAILWAY.
Shanklin to
Shanklin   Shanklin
Portsm'th Har. or Portsm'th Har. or
Southsea (Clar.P.) Southsea (Clar.P.)
PORTSMOUTH HARBOUR or
SOUTHSEA (CLARENCE PIER)
Via Brading, Ryde & S. Rly. Co's. Steamer
THIRD CLASS   THIRD CLASS
Fare 2/9   Fare 2/9
FOR CONDITIONS SEE BACK
7328

2674
SOUTHERN RLY.
CHEAP DAY
Available only as advertised
SHANKLIN to
BEMBRIDGE
via Brading
THIRD CLASS
FOR CONDITIONS SEE BACK

6336
Isle of Wight Ry.
RYDE ESPLANADE
SANDOWN
3rd. CLASS
FOR CONDITIONS SEE BACK

British Railways Board (S)
SANDOWN
PLATFORM TICKET 3d.
Available one hour on day of issue only.
Not valid in trains. Not transferable.
To be given up when leaving platform.
For conditions see over
7544

BRITISH RAILWAYS (S)
This ticket is issued subject to the Bye-laws,
Regulations and Conditions contained in the
Publications and Notices of and applicable to the
Railway Executive.
(S.3) PLATFORM TICKET 1d.
Available ONE HOUR on DAY of ISSUE ONLY.
Not valid in Trains. Not Transferable
SANDOWN
TO BE GIVEN UP WHEN LEAVING PLATFORM
8862

BRITISH RAILWAYS (S)
SHANKLIN
(S.41) PLATFORM TICKET 1d.
Available ONE HOUR on DAY of ISSUE ONLY.
NOT VALID IN TRAINS NOT TRANSFERABLE
To be given up when leaving Platform
FOR CONDITIONS SEE BACK.
6635

Left: **A famous seaside resort but also a changing station for all stops to Newport.**

Super power for this 7.50am Saturdays only double-headed parcel train to Shanklin, seen here approaching Sandown headed by Nos 24 *Calbourne* and 29 *Alverstone* on 10th July 1965.

John Goss

A view taken at the northern end of Sandown station showing an O2 class tank engine shunting a four-coach set. To the left of the train is the sharply curved line which descends towards Alverstone, taking the line on to Merstone and Newport. The double line on the right is the main line to Ryde.

J. R. G. Griffiths

PASSENGERS MUST NOT CROSS THE LINE EXCEPT BY THE SUBWAY

This wooden post lower quadrant signal survived for some years at Sandown after the Second World War. When it was eventually taken down the post ended its days in a railwayman's garden in Newport.

J. R. G. Griffiths

Norman Miller

Both my parents worked on the Island railways. My father's anecdotes are included in *Once Upon a Line... Volume One*, recalling his life as a driver when he regularly drove the now-preserved engines Nos 11 *Newport* and 24 *Calbourne*. My mother, on the other hand, was a Station Mistress at Wootton station on the Isle of Wight Central Railway during the First World War. My mother's name was Dorothy Eva Morey before she was married, and she joined the IWCR at the age of just 19. At the end of the War however, my mother was relieved of her post by former fireman Mr Spinks who had lost an arm while fighting in the trenches on the Western Front. It was during this time that my mother met my father, Cecil William 'Bill' Miller, who was at that time a cleaner-fireman based at Newport shed. My father then lived in 'Fairview', which is now used as the Museum for the Isle of Wight Steam Railway at Haven Street station. Eventually, my parents were married in 1920, and I was born some four years later.

Sandown station in 1929, looking north towards Brading and Ryde. On the left of the picture, a train for Merstone and Newport waits to depart. Note the signal box perched above the canopy on the 'up' platform.

George H. Hunt

It was therefore predictable that I should work on the Island railways. I started work at Sandown station in 1941 after a twelve-month wait. Fred Squibb showed me the ropes and I quickly learnt the job of booking clerk. Not long after this I joined the Royal Air Force, but returned to Sandown in July 1947, working with Bert 'Fruity' Willis. In those days I used to like to go to work at Sandown station quite early, and living in Ryde, I would obtain a ride on the early morning empty coach stock. Working to Shanklin this train was not due to stop at Sandown, as it did not carry any passengers. However, I would ask the driver to slow down to walking pace or pause at Sandown briefly while I climbed off. This practice went well until one morning the driver was one 'Mad' Jack Sturgess on his regular engine, No. 22 *Brading*. I arranged with Jack to slow down to a snail's pace through Sandown for me to climb onto the carriage running board as usual and jump off. As we approached Sandown the train slowed down and Jack watched me climb out ready to jump off onto the platform, but before we entered the station he opened 22's regulator! We passed through the platforms accelerating to something like 30 mph! I made a desperate jump and was lucky not to be killed in the process or break a leg or arm. 'Mad' Jack looked back from the comfort of 22's foot-plate and grinned in delight!

On another occasion I was crossing from the 'down' to the 'up' platform and used the foot-crossing across the line at the Ryde end of Sandown station. It was the end of the day and 'Mad' Jack observed me making my way down the platform to catch his Ryde bound train. As I went to cross the line he opened up 22 and raced towards me on the crossing. The engine snorted steam from under the buffers and I had to dash in front of her to avoid 'Mad' Jack's ploy. Thinking that I was safe, I was then confronted by a jet of water from 22's peep pipe! That was 'Mad' Jack all over and I would always be on my guard when I saw engine 22 *Brading*.

The whole system of cash collection in those days was centred on Newport. If one had to send cash from ticket receipts to Newport it would first be counted and then bagged in a leather pouch. This was then posted into a steel box which was chained to the brake handle of the guard's compartment on Ryde bound trains. Cash dispatches would be placed on the 8am train Monday–Fridays only, but weekend cash receipts were kept in the station safe until Monday morning. The wages were received in the same way and each station had a key to the cash box on the train. These arrived on

the 11am train on a Thursday at Sandown. This arrangement continued until February 1966 when the station at Newport closed.

The most fragile consignment we had to convey were packages of cakes. We regularly dealt with 140 packages. I would live in hope that one would break so that we could consume its contents, but this rarely happened.

After a time I transferred to Newport booking office and stayed there until 1953 when the closures of the Ventnor West and Freshwater lines were in full swing. My next move was to Ryde Esplanade and I stayed there until 1971. In those days Ryde Esplanade was the busiest station on the Isle of Wight. Here we had vast supplies of old Southern Railway tickets well into Nationalisation, and I remember changing the prices on them before they were issued. Mention of tickets reminds me that we were still issuing pre-1923 Isle of Wight Central Railway tickets to various destinations on the Island when at Newport. Had we only have known – it was a collector's paradise!

We used to have some fun at Esplanade station during the summer season. We had Walter Lee down to help out in the enquiry office, and we decided to play a trick on him. We carefully nailed a kipper underneath his desk and after a few days it really started to smell. He didn't discover the origin of the odour and brought in some lavender. He complained that there was a bad smell coming from the toilets. He was only too pleased to return to Bembridge at the end of the season.

A regular feature during the winter and spring at Ryde Esplanade was the terrible gales that caused the sea to blow up through the rails. Such weather conditions could create problems and Ryde Pier was often closed with trains terminating at Esplanade station. Likewise, I have known Ryde Esplanade Tunnel closed with the train service suspended. During the winter months of 1963/64 and again in 1966/67 essential reconstruction work was carried out on Ryde Pier and this involved complete withdrawal of train services between Esplanade and Ryde Pier Head. As a result trains terminated at Esplanade and single-line running was introduced on the 'up' line between St John's Road and Esplanade. Engines were coupled up at both ends of the train as they could not propel trains through the tunnel.

During the summer months, passengers used to leave items of luggage at Esplanade station. To administer this, luggage was sorted into people's names in single or multiple items. This would assist when passengers returned to collect their luggage. One year we had Sammy Wells in Esplanade

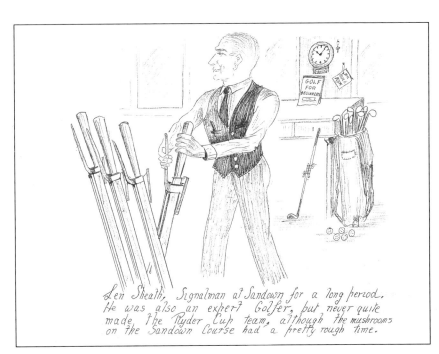

Len Sheath, Signalman at Sandown for a long period. He was also an expert Golfer, but never quite made the Ryder Cup team, although the mushrooms on the Sandown Course had a pretty rough time.

A signalman's view of a train departing from Sandown towards Shanklin in August 1964.

G. M. Kichenside

The 9.20am train to Ventnor double-headed by Nos 17 *Seaview* and 26 *Whitwell* at Sandown on 10th July 1965. On the 'up' platform the crowds of passengers await the next departure for Ryde.

John Goss

On summer Saturdays two 'down' trains from Ryde were double-headed in order to provide locomotives for 'up' trains starting their day's work at Shanklin and Sandown. One of these double-headed trains was the 7.40am Ryde Pier Head–Ventnor, seen here departing from Sandown with engines 26 *Whitwell* and 29 *Alverstone*, on 20th June 1964.

John Goss

No. 32 *Bonchurch* approaches Shanklin station with a six-coach set, which will terminate at Shanklin.   *G. M. Kichenside*

Another famous seaside resort, where, in the fifties, thousands of visitors arrived and departed daily during the summer months.

SHANKLIN

No. 23 *Totland* **approaches Shanklin
with a train for Ventnor.**
The Peter Joyce Collection

station to help out. I recall that the A to J names section was full and when a gentleman called to leave his suitcase Sam informed him that the section was full. However Sammy suggested that he left two or more items as there was still room in this section. The gentleman promptly left the suitcase, his hat and newspaper! Sam had that system so well tuned that summer, the railway must have made a mint!

However, the most amusing anecdote I can tell about my time at Ryde Esplanade involved an enthusiastic railwayman who could not stop watching the passing liners in the Spithead. One day a passenger enquired of this lad, "Where is the urinal young man?" The young porter replied, "It's the one out there with the two red funnels"!

Eventually I transferred to Fishbourne Sealink ferry terminal which was operated and owned by the railway then, but my happiest days at work will always be remembered as watching those little steam trains pass by.

Ted Johnson

I am not originally from the Isle of Wight, but was a signalman on the mainland. I transferred to Shanklin signal box in October 1945 taking over from Ron Hailes who became relief signalman for the Island. The signal box at Shanklin was elevated above the 'up' platform and had a 20-lever frame controlling the passing loop in the station and some sidings.

It was an interesting signal box to work during the summer service as one train an hour terminated at Shanklin in addition to through trains for Wroxall and Sandown. The hourly terminating train normally arrived from Ryde at the same time as an 'up' train from Ventnor and Wroxall. The engine of the 'down' terminating train would then be uncoupled and run forward clear of the loop points, and after the 'up' train had departed it ran through the 'up' platform to reach the other end of its train. The engine then propelled the train to the Wroxall end of the station over Landguard Road bridge, and drew forward into the 'up' platform ready for its return journey back to Ryde. A special small-arm 'Shunt Ahead' signal was provided on the 'down' and 'up' platforms for this shunting arrangement, worked by levers 4 and 17 and they were fitted on the same posts below the starting signals, 3 and 18 levers.

Most of the lines on the Isle of Wight railway system were single track and they needed special signalling to ensure that not more than one train could occupy each section at one time. This was achieved by what were known as electric token instruments, which in steam days on the Island, were provided in each signal box controlling a single-line section. My box at Shanklin controlled two single-line sections: Shanklin to Sandown and Shanklin to Wroxall, hence I had two token instruments to look after. The whole operation of this arrangement is probably best explained by giving an example of working from those days – the section from Shanklin to Wroxall covering the notorious Apse Bank.

Both the signal boxes at Shanklin and Wroxall had a token instrument for the section, which were connected electrically. Inside each instrument were a number of tokens, which were rather like large

Signalman Ted Johnson retrieves a single-line token from the Shanklin signal box electric token instrument, controlling the Shanklin–Sandown section.

G. M. Kichenside

keys about seven or eight inches long. The instruments themselves contained locks which were operated, and thereby opened by, the passage of an electric current through the lock controls. At Shanklin I could only take a token out of the instrument when the lock had been opened electrically by the signalman at Wroxall. A special safety device was added in that if one token had been removed from either instrument at Wroxall or Shanklin it was impossible to obtain a second token, from either instrument, until the first had been put back in either Wroxall or Shanklin's instrument. It follows therefore that if a driver of a train in the Wroxall–Shanklin section had possession of a token he knew that another train could not be in that section at the same time. In steam days signalmen communicated with each other by single stroke bells which were built into the token instruments and we used a special code to indicate different messages. Supposing the Wroxall signalman wanted to send a train down Apse Bank to Shanklin and that the line was clear. The Wroxall signalman would first press his bell tapper which rang the bell in my box at Shanklin, three times in quick succession, then pause and give another one ring. I would therefore hear in my box at Shanklin a three-pause-one bell signal. In the railway signal-

The interior of Shanklin signal box in August 1964, showing the token instrument and lever frame.

G. M. Kichenside

66

ling code language this meant, "Is the line clear for a passenger train between Wroxall and Shanklin?" Given that it was, I would then repeat the bell code back to Wroxall to indicate that the section was clear. As I gave the last ring from Shanklin, I would then hold down the bell tapper for a few seconds and thereby unlock the token instrument at Wroxall, allowing the signalman there to remove a token. When this had been done the Wroxall signalman would give one ring on the bell to me.

The Wroxall signalman could then clear his signals and points for the Shanklin bound train. He would then place the token inside a leather pouch which was attached to a large hoop. If the train stopped at Wroxall he would simply hand it to one of the loco crew, but it it was a non-stopping through train the signalman held the pouch with the hoop in a position so that the driver or fireman could lean out of the cab and put his arm through the hoop and take it with them.

The Wroxall signalman then returned to his box and sent two rings on the bell to me to indicate that the train had entered the single-line section. I would then reply with two rings to show that I had received his message. On arrival at Shanklin I would collect the token in the pouch and place it into my instrument. Next, I would give a two-pause-one beat on the bell to Wroxall which the Wroxall signalman repeated back to me and the Wroxall-Shanklin single line section was once again free.

Prior to using the token system at Shanklin we operated a similar system using electric staffs. These were like a long metal rod with metal rings around them. They were heavy and sometimes hurt your hand when caught from a passing train. I was pleased to see them removed from Shanklin box in the 1950s and replaced with the key token.

For a short period of time I worked temporarily at Cowes and Ventnor signal boxes. I remember that the single-line instruments in Ventnor box sometimes gave false readings which created problems. On one occasion I received a three-pause-two bell code and looked up but thought it was too early for the 10.25am passenger train. I suspected that the approaching train was more likely to be the morning freight from Ryde St John's Road. The train stopped inside Ventnor Tunnel and I set the points for the coal yard and gave three rings on the bell for the waiting train to proceed. As I collected the single-line token from Driver Jim Hunnybun on engine No. 17 *Seaview*, I noticed that he had passenger carriages behind his O2 tank engine. I immediately signalled him to stop, Jim threw over the reversing lever on old 17 and backed her gently into the tunnel again. Meanwhile, I reset the points for number 1 platform. No one was any the wiser officially, and all those involved kept quiet – until now! Nevertheless, Ventnor was a delightful place at which to work.

Likewise I enjoyed a season at Cowes. The regular signalmen there were Larry Woodley and 'Ginger' Watson. The highlight of working there was 'Cowes Week' when tourists swarmed to Cowes to watch the yachts racing in the Solent. Throughout the whole Cowes Week daily newspaper reporters would come up to the station to send off dispatches on the Ryde bound train to their head offices at Fleet Street in London. Although Cowes Week did not officially finish until the following day, the high spot of festivities was the Friday night fireworks display. We would receive several incoming six-coach passenger trains in the evening packed with Islanders and tourists. At the conclusion of the fireworks display it was a mad rush to get the passengers away. Six trains were dispatched from Cowes in just over an hour at ten minute intervals, running non-stop down the single-line section through Mill Hill to Newport, and thence to Ryde, Ventnor, Shanklin or Freshwater. This operation was something to see and believe me, it was a lot of hard work to get them all away on time from Cowes, for all railway staff concerned.

One memory I will always treasure from my time at Cowes was Sunday mornings when we would listen to the hymns played by the brass band of the local Salvation Army. They would play just outside the station, giving it a unique atmosphere, almost like a church.

After my spell away from Shanklin, I was glad to return home again. Here I had greater contact with the two rogue drivers – Nelson Parsons on engine No. 17 *Seaview* and 'Mad' Jack Sturgess on No. 22 *Brading*. These two railway characters were ones you had to watch carefully as they were always up to tricks! One day, after pulling the signals off for Nelson to depart for Wroxall, I set off along the platform to hand him the single-line token. At that moment he whistled up and opened 17's regulator. Realising that he was leaving without the token I sprinted after him and he slammed on the handbrake. "Enjoy your run? I thought you were in training for the Olympics", was his cheeky comment! On another occasion Nelson came in on the 3.20pm from Newport, which went 'around the houses' ie via Merstone. After running around the carriage set, Nelson set off without the Shanklin-Sandown single-line token! I had to send it on in a taxi, but the incident was kept quiet.

The Shanklin–Wroxall electric token instrument in Shanklin signal box in August 1964.

G. M. Kichenside

Signalman Ted Johnson makes a token exchange with a Fratton fireman as he enters Shanklin station in August 1964, on board No. 35 *Freshwater*, with a train bound for Ventnor.

G. M. Kichenside

Sadly, all good things come to an end and I was the last one to operate a steam-hauled train from Shanklin on 31st December 1966. I remember Driver Pete Harbour whistling away on old No. 14 *Fishbourne* and passing over many, many detonators. For the next few months they closed the Ryde Shanklin line for electrification. I was still required to be in Shanklin box each day until they 'opened up' to electric trains in March 1967. I just sat there day after day polishing the instruments or reading newspapers in Shanklin box. It wasn't until just before electrification was completed that I saw a train again. I remember John Townson working engines 31 *Chale* and 24 *Calbourne* into Shanklin on works trains. When they eventually switched on the 'juice', Shanklin signal box was only 'switched in' for peak summer traffic, when both platforms were in use and electric trains were shunted from 'down' to 'up' platforms, using the head shunt at the Wroxall end of the station. Today the signal box has been demolished, but the memories live on, for around me in my retirement, I have many mementoes, including platform seats and the portable gangway from Ventnor station, plus lots of redundant Island signalling equipment.

Len Langborne

I joined the railway in 1959 as Porter at Cowes. My first realisation was that the nowadays somewhat corny word 'brotherhood' really did apply among railwaymen at all levels, and I received many kindnesses from my first day on the railway to my last, and since. Apart from this, an early memory was working at Cowes to the accompaniment of the sound of the prototype 'cup and saucer' hovercraft undergoing trials, and which is now in the Science Museum.

Early in 1960 I moved to Wroxall as porter-signalman, with the strange experience of issuing tickets and operating signalling instruments from the same room. Often, with a queue at the window and a train approaching, the customers would have to take second place for once, and pay at the other end!

At the time, I was working at Wroxall and travelling from Shanklin, whilst Bill Lewis, my opposite number at Shanklin, commuted from Wroxall, so we both applied to do the obvious thing! By late 1960, I was installed at Shanklin.

Summer Saturdays with continuous line occupation and terminating trains were hectic enough, but I remember one day returning to the box with the token from an arriving 'down' train in time to see the fireman furiously shovelling his fire out all over

Shanklin station staff: Left, Porter-Signalman Len Western, right, Station Master Reg Whale.

David Benning

the track! A fusible plug had blown in the engine's firebox, leaving the fireman, the aptly-named Frank Ash, with no alternative. The loads and gradients played havoc with steam pressures and water levels, and a replacement engine was hurriedly sent for. Whilst at Shanklin, I also recall the engine on an 'up' train arriving with its footplate step bent, and covered in hair. The train had hit a straying bullock up the line at Hyde, and having cleared the trains, I walked up the line to find that the unfortunate animal was dead. I then quickly tried to find the gap in the fence, and stop any more cattle getting through.

In 1963 I became a relief signalman, covering Shanklin, Sandown, Brading and Bembridge toll road. This latter duty was far removed from signalling trains, though it made an interesting change and had its lighter moments. It was during this period and a spell back at Shanklin that a visiting goods train decided to celebrate my wife's birthday

No. 32 *Bonchurch* draws forward to run round the terminating train at Shanklin station in August 1964. Note the shunt ahead signal arm has been pulled off although the main home signal remains at danger.

G. M. Kichenside

Opposite page: **A busy commuter station all the year round.**

by its now famous act of depositing its brake van across the main line.

There were sad moments, fortunately few, such as when I was at Sandown, in electrification days when I had to attend the scene of a suicide at Lake. It was bad enough for me, but it must have been harrowing for the poor driver.

My last signal box duty was at Brading, and as I watched the lights of the last train disappear towards Ryde, closed the box and turned off the station gas lamps for the last time, I had a store of pleasant and varied memories to look back on over a comparatively short railway career.

My one regret is that I didn't join the railway a good many years earlier!

This superb panoramic photograph was taken from Cooks Castle in July 1962, and shows an O2 tank hauling an 'up' Ventnor–Ryde Pier Head train away from Wroxall, down the gradient.

H. P. Mason

George Lewis

Just before the outbreak of war in April 1939, I joined the railway, starting at Wroxall station. In those days it was my job as junior to keep the station clean and tidy. There were three others who were senior to me working at Wroxall: Signalmen Bill Cox and Dick Randall and Porter Signalman Alec Widger.

In those days I lived at Whitwell and used to cycle to Ventnor to catch the train to Wroxall. The highlight of the journey was being able to ride on the engine. At the end of the Summer Timetable in September 1939 I was 'stood off', but happily I was able to return to the railway again in February 1940 when I went to Ventnor Town station. This duty involved some work out at Ventnor West station which contrasted well with the Town station, as West was basically a branch line terminal.

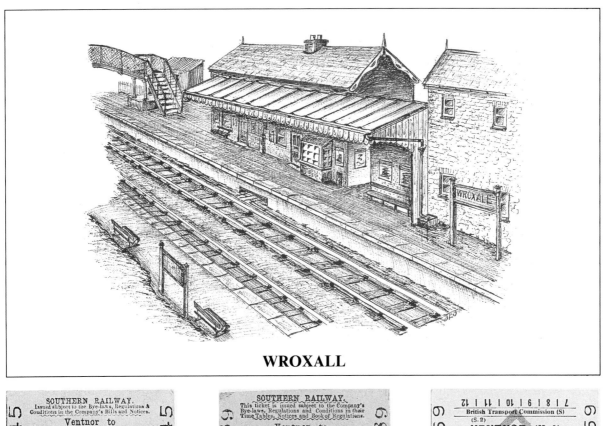

WROXALL

Row 1:

Ticket 1 (2045):
SOUTHERN RAILWAY.
Issued subject to the Bye-laws, Regulations &
Conditions in the Company's Bills and Notices.
Ventnor to
Ventnor / Wroxall
WROXALL
Ventnor / Wroxall
THIRD CLASS   THIRD CLASS
Fare 4½d.   Fare 4½d.
NOT TRANSFERABLE.
2045

Ticket 2 (5389):
SOUTHERN RAILWAY.
This ticket is issued subject to the Company's
Bye-laws, Regulations and Conditions in their
Time Tables, Notices and Book of Regulations.
Ventnor to
Ventnor / Shanklin
SHANKLIN
Ventnor / Shanklin
Third Class (S.68) Third Class
Fare 7d   Fare 7d
5389

Ticket 3 (9559):
7 8 1 6 9 10 11 12
British Transport Commission (S)
(S. 2)
VENTNOR (No.2)
PLATFORM TICKET 2d.
Available one hour on day of issue only.
Not valid in trains. Not transferable.
To be given up when leaving platform.
For conditions see over
1 1 2 3 4 5 6
9559

Row 2:

Ticket 4 (2941):
3rd . SINGLE
Wroxall to
SALISBURY
via
Ryde Portsmouth
Netley Havant
For alternative route rebook of routes
(S) For Conditions as over. Fare 17/3
2941

Ticket 5 (1559):
2nd - SINGLE   SINGLE - 2nd
Ventnor to
Ventnor / Southampton Central or Terminus for Docks   Ventnor / Southampton Central or Terminus for Docks
SOUTHAMPTON CENTRAL or TERMINUS for DOCKS
via Ryde, Portsmouth Harbour & Netley
(S) 1172 / Fare 11/2 (S)
For conditions see over   conditions see over
1559

Ticket 6 (9723):
2nd - SINGLE
Ventnor To
BLACKBURN
Via
For alternative route book of routes
(S) For Conditions over. Fare
9723

Row 3:

Ticket 7 (3069):
S. & I. of W. S. P. Co. Ltd.
VENTNOR
TO
SANDOWN
EXCURSION - SINGLE JOURNEY
INCLUDING ALL PIER TOLLS
Issued subject to conditions printed on
the Company's Time Tables & Bills.
3069

Ticket 8 (1580):
BRITISH RAILWAYS (S)
Privilege Single
Valid Three Days
Ventnor to
Ryde St Johns Rd
Via
THIRD CLASS FARE
FOR CONDITIONS SEE BACK.
1580

Ticket 9 (1439):
ONE DOG [ACCOMPANYING PASSENGER]
Wroxall to
ANY STATION IN THE LoW. NOT
EXCEEDING 3 MILES DISTANT
(S)   Rate 0/3
For conditions see over
1439

Row 4:

Ticket 10 (5575):
2nd - SINGLE   SINGLE - 2nd
Wroxall to
Wroxall / Ryde Pier Head   Wroxall / Ryde Pier Head
RYDE PIER HEAD
via Brading
(S)   3/3 Fare 3/3   (S)
For conditions see over   For conditions see over
5575

Ticket 11 (12956):
2nd - CHEAP DAY   CHEAP DAY - 2nd
Shanklin to   Wroxall to
WROXHALL   SHANKLIN
(S)   (S)
For conditions see over   For conditions see over
12956

Ticket 12 (15860):
2nd - SINGLE   SINGLE - 2nd
Wroxall to
Wroxall / Shanklin   Wroxall / Shanklin
SHANKLIN
(S)   9d. Fare 9d.   (S)
For conditions see over   For conditions see over
15860

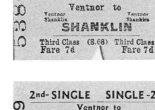

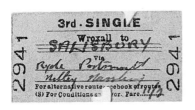

These were happy days for me working at Ventnor, but a bit hair raising at times with the war coming right to our door step. One day, almost without warning, the German Luftwaffe suddenly descended from the clouds and attacked the Ventnor Radar Station located on the top of St Boniface Down, high above the station. I vividly remember the bombs whistling down on the pylons and running for cover in the caves in Ventnor station yard. These caves had been converted into an air raid shelter, but we never believed that on the sunny Isle of Wight they would ever be put to any use. Being young, I was more interested in the aircraft and their bombing exploits than going into the shelter and I was stunned by Hitler's war machine as it left death and destruction, just above the station.

The Station Master overseeing Ventnor Town

A busy scene at Wroxall in August 1964, showing an approaching train entering the station from Shanklin, while No. 32 *Bonchurch* prepares to depart as soon as the line is clear.
G. M. Kichenside

No. 26 *Whitwell* draws to a halt at Wroxall station, following the gruelling climb up Apse Bank.
G. M. Kichenside

Signalman Dick Randall has just collected the single-line token from Fireman Charlie Hackett who is pictured looking from the footplate of No. 35 *Freshwater*. The driver at the controls of this engine is John Townson, who is out of picture, applying the Westinghouse brakes.

Mike Esau

and West stations was Mr Bill Bennett, whose son was Signalman Ron Bennett at Newport 'B' signal box. Bill Bennett's hobby was repairing clocks and he had a garage in the station yard at Ventnor. If he was not to be found in his office, you knew where he was – in the garage repairing clocks. There was only one snag with the situation in that if you were ever late for work you dare not say your alarm did not go off, as Bill would turn around and tell you to bring it in to him for repair.

The staff at Ventnor Town in those days were all very friendly and included Signalmen Sid Sartin

Relief Signalman Ray Draper pictured at Wroxall signal box on 4th June 1960. The signal box and booking office at Wroxall were located on the 'up' platform, within the station building. Ray Draper's reminiscences are contained in *Once Upon a Line ... Volume Two*.

H. P. Mason

No. 24 *Calbourne* waits at Wroxall for the single-line section to Ventnor, as another O2 clears this section with an 'up' train. Note the carriage the destination board with the inscription, 'Ryde, Sandown, Shanklin, Ventnor'. These destination boards could be purchased from Ryde Works in 1966 for one shilling each – today's equivalent of five new pence.

The Peter Joyce Collection

and Bert Tosdevin, Porters Harold Fry and Jim Gladdis, Clerks Alf Westmore and Bill Baxter, with John Duff and myself as juniors. John Duff was always full of fun and games and I recall one amusing incident when working at West station. John was struggling down the line with a bundle of sticks on his back, which he had cut in the nearby woods. As he stumbled along the platform who should he bump into but Station Master Bill Bennett. "What are you doing with them Duffy?" enquired the Station Master. "I have just been and got them for a driver Sir," replied a surprised John Duff. "Well, you had better go and cut some for me!" demanded Mr Bennett. So back young John had to go, with sweat still dripping from his brow,

Shanklin station staff: left to right are, George Lewis, Fred Welham and Summer Season Temporary Porter Norman.

David Benning

from the first visit to the woods.

In 1948 I was promoted to signalman at Ventnor box. Ventnor signal box was like a restaurant in the mornings, as I well remember, with Guard Stan Jacobs, who was often on the early morning mail train, coming up to the box for his breakfast. In fact, it became so frequent that a charge of sixpence a week was made for tea and breakfast – where else would this happen but on the Isle of Wight railways?

After a few years at Ventnor I moved to Shanklin where I stayed for seven years before moving on again and off the Island for promotion to Worting Junction, leaving my brother Bill behind at Wroxall.

Des Boynton

Towards the end of the Second World War I joined the Southern Railway as a clerk at Ventnor in January 1945. I worked there until the railway closed in April 1966. As a booking clerk it was my job to issue tickets and collect them, load and unload parcels from the trains, working six days a week, totalling 48 hours in all.

In steam days Ventnor station was a beautiful location to work, with steep cliffs at the side of the station containing many caves which were used by local coal merchants. The overhanging vegetation provided nesting for all sorts of birds, magpies and rooks mostly. Their constant chatter mingled with the sound of the locomotive Westinghouse pumps and was a feature of the station atmosphere in those days.

I spent a short time working on the relief staff before returning back to Ventnor. During this period on the relief staff I was sent out to Bembridge for the day. This was a complete disaster for me as the guard came up to me in the evening and

No.33 *Bembridge* barks away from Wroxall towards Ventnor on 7th August 1965, with Driver Gerald Coombes at the regulator.

Tony Scarsbrook

Terminus station of the old Isle of Wight Railway Company.

VENTNOR

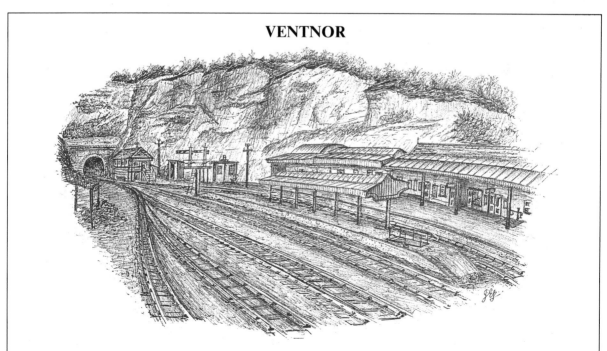

said, "It's a bit dark outside". Apparently it was my job to light the station gas lights, but no one had informed me of my duties. Likewise I was surprised to have people come up and ask to purchase barrow loads of sand. I was astonished to hear that sand was owned by the railway in Bembridge. Likewise a spell at Newport station revealed that one of the railway station staff operated his own insurance business from the station premises – purely on a private commercial basis! Lots of people used to come up to the booking office with their premiums. I had no idea what they were on about! After spending a year working at Shanklin I was glad to return home to Ventnor.

A pre-war picture of Ventnor station photographed from St Boniface Down. This photograph, taken from the 'down' side of the line, shows the caverns and caves used as offices and stores, and the sidings in full use. On the platform, waiting to be loaded onto the train, is an assortment of milk churns and passenger luggage in advance.

J. R. G. Griffiths

No. 28 *Ashey* has just arrived at Ventnor with the 5.18pm Ryde–Ventnor train on platform 2, whilst on platform 1, a Ryde bound train prepares to depart. Passengers from the terminating train are seen making their way across the portable gangway which was the only means of access to the centre island platform at Ventnor right up to the station's closure in 1966. Note also the display board, right, advertising cheap tickets to Chichester for motor racing at Goodwood.

H. P. Mason

Signalman Syd Sartin hands the single-line token hoop to Driver Eddie Prangnell on his regular engine, O2 class No. 21 *Sandown*.
Ron H. Childs

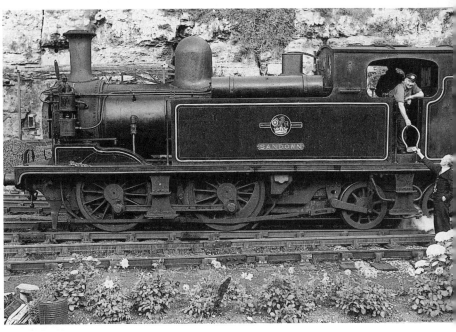

The smiling face of Signalman Syd Sartin of Ventnor, pictured standing at the top of the steps at Ventnor signal box. In 1961 Syd reckoned that he had signalled 15,000 trains during his 26 years working at this box. Syd however, commenced his railway service at Winchfield and afterwards served at many stations on the Southern Region including Clapham Junction. To the hundreds of railway enthusiasts who visited Ventnor, he will be remembered with warmth and affection as the smiling signalman with an open invitation to visit him in the box.

Mrs J. M. Williets Collection

BY J.E.J.

Mr Sydney Sartin

FOR DETAILS. —

APPLY WHITEHALL 1212

OR ANY PUBLIC ESTABLISHMENT

WHERE ALCOHOLIC BEVERAGES ARE SERVED.—

Having run round its train, No. 31 *Chale* eases slowly forward onto the Ryde end of the carriage set. Driver Maurice Prouten is at the controls and *Chale* has left a curtain of steam across the tunnel mouth to mask the signal box at Ventnor.

John A. Britton

I stayed at Ventnor until it closed in April 1966. The final week before we closed it was hectic in that we sold just about all our tickets to collectors wishing to purchase a cheap souvenir of Ventnor. The cheap tickets to Wroxall sold out first, the child tickets, followed by the adult tickets, then the platform tickets and so on. I ended up not having a souvenir to keep for myself, but whenever I want to be reminded of the old days I pay a visit to Haven Street and have a ride behind, No. 24 *Calbourne* or No. 8 *Freshwater*.

Tony H. Edmunds

My reminiscences continue from those recalled in *Volume Two* of *Once Upon a Line...* with my next job at Ryde Pier Head.

Wally Lown Jr and Sid Young were booking clerks and Roger Bartrum and I were middle turn learners covering as required when either of the seniors was absent. Fred Hallett and Walt Marks were station foremen, Claud Orchard and Jack Daish cranemen, Fred Bartlett and Arthur Tosdevin, sometimes Bill (Major) Moore and later Norman Brealy, auto-drivers, and Taffy Beynon, Les Smith, Frank Godsell and later George Jenvey ticket collectors. Hilda Brett (now Smith) managed the refreshment room.

Whilst at Esplanade during the War there was much conjecture upon the outcome should the pier be attacked and severed, and as I went into the parcels office at the Pier Head for the first time, the bullet hole through the door frame did little to convince me that this was not exactly unlikely! However I need not have worried; perhaps the

Luftwaffe viewed the pair of ancient Lewis guns in the sand-bagged emplacement atop the Round House and decided that discretion was the better part of valour. In any event it transpired that this ominous defensive capability, backed up by the four-man multi-service RTO unit commanded by F/Sgt Bill Williams, was sufficient to hold this most vulnerable of outposts against the might of the Third Reich.

Variety was truly the spice of life at the Pier Head; for instance, it was one of our duties to levy mooring fees and landing charges on a variety of craft from all branches of the services. RAF crash boats, naval craft of all descriptions, Army landing barges and even the naval motor launches built at Woodnut's yard at St Helens were all logged and the charges invoiced. It was a thankless task, and the abuse to which one was occasionally subjected did not give one the feeling of exactly contributing to the war effort. To try to obtain and write on a clip-board the registered gross tonnage etc. of some trifling little liberty boat, whilst all and sundry were being blown all over the place on a rainy night in black-out conditions could hardly be called the easiest way of ensuring that a few paltry shillings went into the Southern Railway coffers. Even the landing barges which embarked the Canadians (then in camp in Whitefield Woods near Ryde) for Dieppe were meticulously recorded, but when some of those same barges returned with what was left of their original cargo, our enthusiasm for this particular aspect of our working day really took a dive. Seldom were these charges paid without query, and it sometimes happened that a small boat captain was inadvertently 'dropped in it' by paying an unofficial visit to Ryde in order to enjoy a doubtless well-deserved 'rub down with the Sporting Life', only to have the plot blown by an over-zealous railwayman at Ryde Pier Head who recorded his boat as having been tied up there for a couple of hours, when it should have been elsewhere.

Charlie Box was not an employee, but was nonetheless of considerable importance to the welfare of all staff in the booking office. He was in fact a naval despatch rider who brought from Cowes each day a most official looking heavily sealed white canvas bag addressed to the C. in C. Portsmouth which we signed for and 'value waybilled' onward. As far as we were concerned this was only a minor part of Charlie's war effort – of greater significance was the apparently inexhaustible supply of naval cigarettes, tobacco and other almost unobtainable goodies which he brought in.

Albert Watson, many feared, would suffer permanent deformity. Not that animosity could be borne towards him from any quarter – it was simply that he spent so much time standing on the Pier Head station looking up under the platform canopies supervising his gang of lady painters that he seemed in danger of being 'stuck' in that position. These half-dozen, including Mrs Graham, Mrs France and Lena Bessant, worked terribly hard chipping and banging away, and putting on gallons of green and stone coloured paints. They operated from a goods van positioned on the blocks at platform 1 which served as a mess room and paint store. To say that they terrified us junior clerks was an understatement; unmentionable threats were often made to us and there was no doubt in our minds that even if only by sheer weight of numbers, they were capable of carrying them out.

My working progress was being monitored, and what T. F. Thompson saw obviously gave no cause for pleasure. As a last resort he wrote a letter of entreaty to my mother suggesting that I would be well advised to heed the dictates of HRH the Duke of Edinburgh, or words to that effect. T.F.T. and my mother were similarly natured, both being kindly and kind souls, yet by no means soft, and capable of delivering stern judgement when such was warranted. In the course of exchange of letters, which I was not privileged to read, it became obvious that a considerable rapport built up between them, although as far as I am aware they never met. Quite regularly I passed regards one to the other, and it would not be unfair to say that T.F.T. was most highly regarded by mother for taking such interest as to try to make a railwayman

out of me. "And how is that dear Mr Thompson?" she would ask occasionally.

I now know that there are little 'domestic ceremonies' peculiar to some industries. Apprentice coopers at Whitbreads London brewery were tarred and feathered and young boat builders received the red lead treatment. For the young entrants deemed to have offended in the CME's or loco departments, it was a similar routine, but with axle grease, and for me, the lady painters had decreed, it was to be the application of the station name stamp. Suspecting nothing I went from the booking office to the parcels office one lunchtime, and was promptly grabbed by several members of the uniformed staff ('les fils' in attendance) and it wasn't until the situation became critical – they got as far as trying to unfasten my belt – that I resorted to some pretty rigorous action and managed to free myself, but not before the villain with the station stamp had aimed in the right direction but only succeeded in impressing it on my light grey flannels. It wasn't long before my mother wanted to know what had happened; after all it wasn't everybody who went around with 'Southern Railway Ryde Pier Head, May 1943' on the fly of his trousers. There was nothing for it, but the truth to which my mother listened, with a look of increasing disgust. "And where" she said, "was that nice Mr Thompson when all this went on?" How at the age of 16 does one try to convince one's mother that it's a man's world?

I had heard of G. H. R. Gardener, the Assistant Divisional Superintendant, but had not seen or met him. One morning at Ryde Pier Head the booking office door suddenly burst open and in strode a figure clad in a black overcoat with close cropped hair. The conversation went something like this:

Intruder: Will you cash me a cheque?
Edmunds: (Resenting the intrusion into his sanctum) Certainly not! We're not allowed to.

Enter Walt Marks, station foreman.

Marks: Good Morning, Mr Gardener.
Gardener: Good morning, Walter.
Edmunds: (Red-faced) How much was your cheque to be for?
Gardener: Can you manage thirty shillings? (Cheque bearing G.H.R.G.'s rather flamboyant signature, duly cashed.) I shall need this for my journey. I've been called up and have to report tomorrow at Bury St Edmunds. Can you give me some train times out of London?

Edmunds: (Picking up the GWR timetable.) Certainly, sir.
Gardener: (After watching Edmunds floundering hopelessly.) It's in this one. (Picks up LMS timetable with similar result.)
Edmunds: There is an ABC at the Esplanade.
Gardener: Good. I'll call in there on my way back to Newport.

I saw him but once thereafter in the uniform of a 2nd Lieutenant in, I think, the Royal Engineers. His successor was a Mr Nicholson.

Quite without warning I was put to work in Sandown booking office and on relief conditions at that. 'Eureka'! My g.n.p. almost doubled, taking into account expenses. The staff were Signalmen Roland Gallop and Jack Healy, Alf Cammel, Porter-Signalman Jim Foster, Porter Peter Simmonds, a junior porter, and Doris Russell in the office. Station Master Harold (Fishy) Attrill and I did not enjoy even the vaguest rapport. He would arrive each morning with a rose in his buttonhole, swing a creaky right arm onto the desk to sign whatever was required, while smoking an absolutely foul pipe which usually had saliva dripping from the underside of the bowl. The 'creaky' right arm was apparently due to a war wound which necessitated the wearing of a hinged support and it was this that emitted a sound of varying volume, often similar to that of a bicycle with a rusty chain being ridden hard up-hill. It seemed that the louder the creak the more Harold would 'ride' me. He read the riot act to me one day over some foul misdemeanour, and at the end of his spluttering tirade, remarked that I was the most useless railwayman he had come across in all his years of service. My riposte was that I entirely agreed with all that he had said and felt therefore that it was quite pointless in the circumstances that we should both worry about it! His face became purple with rage and he dropped his pipe which broke into two pieces.

Transport to work on early turn and home after late turn, unless one was lucky enough to be able to get the last train, was by bicycle. It was not uncommon to arrive at a station as drowned as the proverbial rat. On one such morning I fought an uneven battle with the elements between Bembridge and Sandown. The wind was gale-force from the south-west, the rain horizontal, and my head low over the handlebars. There had been considerable military activity in the vicinity of Brown's Golf Course, and I suddenly realised that not only had I pulled up just short of a barbed-wire road block, but was looking down the barrel of a sentry's rifle. It soon became clear that this rather

wet and bad-tempered fellow had not the slightest intention of appreciating the importance of my journey; he was not going to let me through and there was nothing for it but to divert and go to Sandown via Brading. This route became the norm as, despite trying to get a pass from the military authorities to cycle along Sandown Front, they considered, perhaps not without good reason, that the security connected with PLUTO, ('Pipeline Under The Ocean') so critical in the subsequent invasion of Normandy, was more important than some minor inconvenience to the junior booking clerk at the local station.

Security was also, in retrospect, a major consideration when over the telephone came the news that a special train had left Ryde Pier Head which would travel non-stop and terminate at Sandown. Before the news could really be assimilated signal bells were clanging, a six-coach set had pulled in and a battalion of American infantry were milling around all over the station. After getting them into some order their CO, one Captain McCann came into the parcels office and asked to use the telephone, a perfectly reasonable request, on the grounds that he and his troops had arrived but that day in Southampton from America, been trained, boated and conveyed to Sandown but had little idea what should happen next. Despite all his tribulations McCann had not reckoned with the Commandments According to St Fishy (Attrill) the first of which was, "Thou shalt not use the Post Office telephone unless it be to notify consignees of the arrival of perishables".

With the best will in the world Doris Russell, booking clerk, reviewed the situation; none of the essential ingredients needed to fulfil the requirements of the First Commandment was present so that she might find in McCann's favour. He and his men had certainly arrived by train, but they were not smothered in parcel stamps, consigned to anyone in particular, nor by the wildest stretch of the imagination could he or his troops be considered perishable. Accordingly he was directed to the public telephone box.

Another officer came into the parcels office, reported the public box out of order, and again asked to use the station 'phone, which I permitted. He made three calls, the last of which elicited the information that the battalion's destination was the Trouville Hotel. Doris Russell was furious; not only had I broken the First Commandment, but had no idea of the cost of the calls, which, after another carpeting from Fishy, I estimated to be £1 3s 6d, and having made out a bill-head for this amount (which must have contained a plus contingency factor of about 300%), called at the Trouville Hotel, not without some misgivings. I need not have worried; the money was duly collected, to the grudging surprise of some and considerable profit to myself – the Americans were more than generous with their candy and cigarettes which I felt justified in retaining for personal use as some small compensation for pain and suffering resulting from three measly telephone calls.

At Bembridge Mrs Bartrum had been succeeded by John Orchard, who in turn joined the RAF, and I was sent to fill the vacancy on the opposite turn to Charlie Wetherick, a porter whose exact grade I forget. Walter Buckett and Alf Dallimore were guards on the branch, and Alf's son Brian, recently appointed personnel director of W. H. Smith & Son, managed the book stall. Peter Hyett and Tony Abbott were junior porters at St Helens.

Walter Lee was still sick and living in the station house with his wife who did not enjoy particularly good health either. The last member of a somewhat decrepit triumvirate was an Airedale dog who, by application of the 1:7 ratio must have been about 200 years old. There were great black protuberances hanging from this wretched animal that Walter took for a walk each evening when both were able, but when not, he simply opened his front door and let it out onto the platform.

That platform was God's chosen acre for Charlie Wetherick. He swept it, whitewashed the edges and all other places that blackout conditions required, including the platform roof supports, which was the area polluted on occasions by Walter's dog before it hobbled back through the door being held open for it. The pollution had to be disinfected, the disinfectant destroyed the effect of the whitewash and Charlie was not best pleased!

Serious situations sometimes require drastic remedies. One day Charlie, armed with the cane-bristled broom with which he kept his platform so pristine, waited in the booking hall peeping around the corner. Sure enough the dog appeared, padded down the platform, came to its favourite post, turned around and cocked its leg. Charlie lunged with the accuracy of a highly-trained infantry man with a bayonet. The dog took off with a yelp straight up the platform and past the door being held open for it by Walter, whose face must have been an absolute study. Walter got the message, so perhaps did the dog, although Charlie denied any involvement.

Bembridge as a station was not without interest. It wasn't every station that had a turntable or a toll road. The turntable was a source of great enjoyment to Brian Dallimore and myself. Often we

would unlock it, get it revolving at a considerable speed and then use it as a merry-go-round by draping ourselves over the locking handles. On one occasion we just had time to cease activities before the train arrived and our haste almost led to disaster. It was only the eagle eye of Driver Bill Miller who looked down from the footplate and noticed that the turntable was set to cover the runround track instead of the main. He gave his fireman a rocket for failing to set it correctly on the previous run. If the poor innocent fireman did not learn a lesson, Brian and I certainly did!

The tollgate was manned by ticket collector Bill Cranwell, an asthmatic who had been transferred from the London area for health reasons, and by Roly Townson when he wasn't working the crane – his primary occupation – at St Helens Quay. Another tollgate duty was to levy a charge collectable per cubic yard of sand removed from the beach, but I don't think that this was taken very seriously, the odd sixpence being paid in hardly being worth the effort. However, earlier in the century the sources of revenue were more varied, and charges for landings at St Helens were strictly controlled. It is perhaps worthy of note that the Southern Railway bye-laws were not enacted until late in the year 1935. Under the requirements of Clause 15/2 of the Act, the 'Old' Company was bound to 'dredge an area of not less than five acres of the harbour adjoining Bembridge to a depth of not less than nine feet at low water', and this was maintained by the Southern Railway by virtue of the dredger *The Ballaster*, skippered by 'Mulligan' Burden, with George Bartlett and 'Bat' Dyer as crew. Another duty of Mulligan's was to operate the sluice gates which, on the ebb tide, released water from the River Yar. When the harbour was sold in 1963, *The Ballaster* was also disposed of and, I think, worked finally on the River Medina.

The harbour was quite full of small landing-craft immediately prior to 'D' Day. As it was one of my duties, when on early turn at Bembridge, to go each day to St Helens to check the books, (which was nonsense as both junior porters, Peter Hyett and Tony Abbott were far more capable than I), Stan Martin asked me to let him know the number of barges that were actually alongside the quay on this day in particular. I wandered along the quay, counted thirteen and was walking back to my bike when I noticed that an Army welder doing a repair from outside one of these craft had burned through the side of it and had ignited a tarpaulin which was burning away, revealing that the cargo was an awful lot of rather large artillery shells. I shouted at him but the hiss from the welding torch prevented

A.D. 1896.

SECOND SCHEDULE.

Goods Rates.

	s.	d.
Ale beer and porter per 54 gallons	0	6
Ale (bottled) per cwt.	0	4
Ale (bottled) per dozen bottles	0	1
Anchors per cwt.	0	9
Anchor stock per foot run	0	2
Bark per ton	2	0
Beef or pork per cwt.	0	3
Biscuit or bread per cwt.	0	3
Blubber per ton of 252 gallons	3	0
Bones and bone dust per ton	1	6
Bottles per gross	0	9
Bricks per thousand	1	6
Butter and lard per cwt.	0	9
Cables iron or hempen per ton	3	0
Canvas per bolt	0	1
Casks (empty) not being returned packages each	0	3
Cattle:		
Bulls cows and oxen each	3	0
Calves each	1	0
Horses each	4	0
Pigs each	0	6
Sheep each	1	0
Chalk per ton	1	0
Cheese per cwt.	0	4
Chimney pots each	0	3
Clay per ton	1	0
Cloth haberdashery &c. per package not exceeding a cwt.	0	6
Carriages:		
Chaises or other four-wheeled carriages each	7	6
Gigs carts and other two-wheeled carriages each	5	0
Hand carts and perambulators each	1	0
Coals per ton	1	0
Copper per ton	3	0
Cordage per cwt.	0	3
Cork per cwt.	0	6
Crystal per cwt.	0	6
Dogs each	0	6
Drugs (in casks hampers or boxes) per cubic foot	0	2
Earthenware (in casks hampers or boxes) per cubic foot	0	2
Eggs per cwt.	0	6
Fish (dried and salted) per cwt.	0	3
Fish fresh (not enumerated) per cwt.	0	2

	s.	d.	A.D. 1896
Flax per ton	2	0	
Flour and meal per cwt.	0	9	
Fruit per bushel	0	4	
Furniture (household) per 5 cubic feet	0	4	
Glass per ton	1	5	
Grains and seeds per quarter	0	6	
Groceries (not enumerated) per cwt.	0	6	
Guano per ton	1	6	
Gunpowder per 100 lbs.	1	0	
Hams bacon or tongues per cwt.	0	4	
Hardware per ton	2	6	
Hares and rabbits per dozen	0	4	
Hay per ton	1	6	
Hemp per ton	2	0	
Herrings (fresh) per thousand	0	3	
Herrings (cured) per cwt.	0	3	
Hides:			
Ox cow or horse (wet or dry) each	0	2	
Iron:			
Bar bolt rod and shots per ton	1	6	
Pig and old per ton	1	0	
Manufactured per ton	2	6	
Pots each	0	1	
Kelp per ton	2	0	
Lead per ton	2	6	
Leather (tanned and dressed) per cwt.	0	3	
Lime per 28 bushels	1	4	
Limestone per ton	1	0	
Machinery per ton	2	6	
Manure (not enumerated) per ton	1	0	
Masts and spars 10 inches in diameter and upwards each	4	6	
Masts and spars under 10 inches	3	0	
Meat (fresh) per cwt.	0	6	
Milk per gallon	0	0½	
Musical instruments per cubic foot	0	1	
Nets per 5 cubic feet	0	4	
Oakum per cwt.	0	2	
Oils per ton	2	0	
Oilcake per ton	2	0	
Oranges and lemons per box	0	6	
Ores per ton	1	0	
Oysters per bushel	0	3	
Paint per cwt.	0	4	
Pitch and tar per cwt.	0	6	
Potatoes per cwt.	0	2	
Poultry and game per dozen	0	4	
Rags and old rope per ton	2	0	

him from hearing so I hurled a handful of ballast at him, pointed at the fire and shot off like the proverbial 'robber's dog'.

I'm not suggesting that the village of St Helens was saved from destruction by a handful of ballast, but at least it saved the welder from the possibility of a nasty shock!

Charlie Wetherick was prone to irascibility with his colleagues, but not with the Bembridge 'gentry' before whom he could be servile to the point of exasperation to those around him. His *modus operandi* was simple – as soon as anything unaccompanied arrived at the station addressed to one of the 'big houses' he would ensure that it did not get included in the carrier's (Preston's) round, then ring up the consignee a couple of trains later, explain that the parcel had just arrived and as it was undoubtedly urgent he would be pleased to arrange delivery himself. It worked like a charm! It was beneath his dignity to speak to anyone other than the head of the house; even the butler to him was an inferior being. The result was that there were often mysterious envelopes delivered to the station by hand bearing Charlie's name and at Christmas the booking office resembled Aladdin's Cave with pheasants, chickens and other goodies as rewards for his assiduous service to the donors.

Perhaps it was because Charlie was usually a shade 'crusty' that he was the subject of the odd practical joke. Roly Townson was not beyond putting a wad of oily waste on top of the tortoise stove as he was leaving the office on a winter's night after paying in his tollgate cash. The result can be imagined, but it was Driver Jack Sturgess who was Charlie's absolute *bête noire*!

When on early turn, living in St Helens, Charlie rode to Bembridge on the light engine which waited at St Helens station after shunting the Quay. He would walk down the hill, tea-can over arm, and leisurely filling his first pipe of the day. A few minutes before he was due to arrive Sturgess would blow the whistle and open the regulator without moving the engine more than a little. Charlie would appear breathless less he missed his lift and soaked in slopped tea, whereupon Sturgess would wait a further ten minutes before setting off for Bembridge.

Walter Lee returned to duty in early 1945. He was a true railwayman in every sense, using every free pass and privilege ticket order that he could get

A.D. 1896.		s.	d.
Sails per cwt.		0	6
Salt per cwt.		0	1
Sand per ton		1	0
Shrimp baskets each		0	2
Skins:			
Calf goat sheep lamb or dog per dozen		0	6
Slates per ton of 24 cubic feet		2	0
Spirits per gallon		0	1
Stones per ton of 16 cubic feet		1	6
Steel per ton		3	0
Sugar per cwt.		0	3
Tallow soap and candles per cwt.		0	3
Tea per cwt.		1	0
Tiles per thousand		1	6
Tin and zinc per ton		3	0
Tobacco per cwt.		1	6
Turbot per score		0	3
Turnips per ton		0	6
Turpentine and varnish per cwt.		0	6
Turtle each		2	6
Vegetables (not enumerated) per cwt.		0	4
Vinegar per 54 gallons		0	6
Wine per 54 gallons		1	0
Wine (bottled) per dozen bottles		0	2
Wood:			
Fir pine and other descriptions not enumerated per load of 50 feet		1	6
Oak or wainscot per load of 50 feet		2	0
Firewood per 216 cubic feet fathom		1	6
Laths and lathwood per fathom of 216 cubic feet		2	6
Handspikes per one hundred and twenty		3	0
Oars per one hundred and twenty		5	0
Spars under 22 feet in length above 2½ and under 4 inches in diameter per one hundred and twenty		5	0
Spars 2½ inches in diameter and under per one hundred and twenty		4	0
Spars 22 feet in length and upwards and not exceeding 4 inches in diameter per one hundred and twenty		9	0
Spars above 4 and under 6 inches in diameter per one hundred and twenty		14	0
Spokes of wheels not exceeding 2 feet in length per one hundred and twenty		2	0
Spokes of wheels exceeding 2 feet in length per one hundred and twenty		3	0
Trenails per thousand		2	6
Wedges per thousand		2	6
Pipe staves and others in proportion per one hundred and twenty		2	6
Lignum vitæ fustic logwood mahogany and rosewood per ton		2	0
Wool per cwt.		0	4
Yarn per cwt.		0	2

his hands on, and using ambulance days for the benefit of St John for which cause he would collect alms on occasion, resplendent in the uniform of what might, in Gilbertian terms, be described as that of a modern major-general. (No offence intended.)

Let Walter not be derided. His knowledge of the railway network of the whole of Great Britain was vast and there was hardly a line upon which he had not travelled and held some memory for him, but it was the Brading to Bembridge branch which held his complete affection to the extent that a 'single to Brading' covered, in his opinion, only half the pleasures available for very little extra financial outlay. On receiving a request for such a ticket, the conversation, particularly if late on a Saturday evening, would be similar to the following:

Passenger: A single to Brading, please.

Walter: (In his sing-song voice) Only a single, friend?

Passenger: Yes, just a single.

Walter: But it's a lovely journey, you know, and you would enjoy a return trip.

Passenger: Look here, mate, give me a bloody ticket to Brading 'cos I live there and I don't want to end up back 'ere!

Walter: Ah, well, what a pity. You're missing a lot, you know. That will be tuppence ha'penny, please.

Such dedication should not be challenged.

Many a child of my generation was bounced upon mother's knee to what might be truly termed 'the station song'. It was to my knowledge unique to Bembridge, although it could also, and here I suppose I risk invoking a state of war, have applied to St John's Road. The words and following setting are totally original, and with regard to the latter I thank my friend Everard Charlton.

Down at the station
Early in the morning
See the little puffer trains
All in a row.
Along comes Mr Vallender
Turns his little handle,
Choo-choo Brading
Off we go.

Who knows whether it was Percy or Bill whose fame is thus commemorated but whichever, they would hardly have appreciated their beloved engines being called 'choo-choos'. Perhaps even in the innocent cause of infant happiness there were depths which should never have been plumbed.

There were pleasant little 'quirks' associated with Bembridge station; for instance, although the Pilot Boat Inn and the Marine Hotel, (now the Row Barge) were about thirty yards apart on the other side of the road from the station yard, the guard, once the train was made ready for departure, never darkened the door of the latter nor the engine crew the former. It was not that antipathy existed, but simply that the quickest route to the nearest pub was of paramount importance.

There could not have been many stations with a 'two minute' bell. Although I did not hear it rung in anger, apparently it was used two minutes before the departure of each train to warn intending passengers coming down the hill that they had that amount of time available and no more. Presumably its use ended with the on-set of war, but this one foot high historic brass bell was truly part of the furniture, fixtures and fittings and deserving of preservation for posterity.

And so, upon Walter Lee's return from sickness I returned to Ryde Pier Head and performed relief duties until March 1945, when the Army insisted that it had prior call on my services, and it was not until 1948 that I returned and attempted to assimilate the changes brought about by Nationalization.

Chapter Two – The Brading Harbour Branch (Brading–Bembridge)

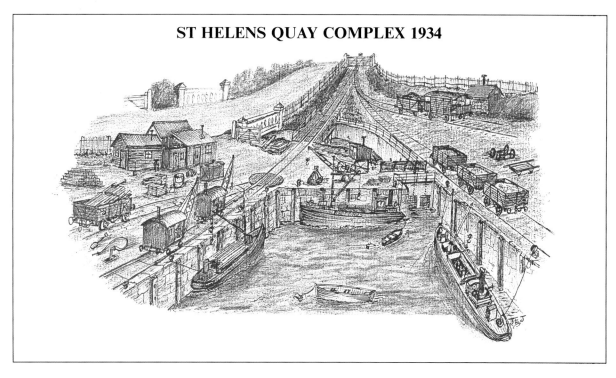

ST HELENS QUAY COMPLEX 1934

At this time St Helens Quay was a busy and prosperous port; most of the main carriers used it to load and unload their goods. The Southern had two steam cranes operating and their own dredger called the *Ballaster*, that dredged the shingle used as track ballast, was always berthed here. In later years, Medina Wharf became the chief port in the Island for railway materials, and Newport was used by the carriers; and so it was that the facilities of St Helens faded into insignificance.

ST HELENS

Like most Island village stations, badly situated from the centre of local activities, and bus operators took full advantage.

Vic Hailes, standing on the flood-light yard ladder at St Helens Quay in 1937.

J. R. G. Griffiths

85

Above: **Vic Hailes poses for the camera of Joe Griffiths on the transfer crane at St Helens Quay. This crane had, hours before, unloaded an Adams O2 boiler brought over from Southampton Docks.**

J. R. G. Griffiths

Opposite page: **No. 15 Cowes at Bembridge station. Could the exceptionally clean appearance of this engine be the result of Dan Wheeler's handy work?**

J. R. G. Griffiths

Right: **The newly imported Adams O2 boiler from Eastleigh Works bound for Ryde Works, pictured at St Helens Quay. The boiler, incidently, according to Vic Hailes, was painted in red oxide primer.**

J. R. G. Griffiths

Left: **Vic Hailes shows Joe Griffiths the working of the Quay Road siding on the bridge across the River Yar at St Helens Quay. In the background, right, can be seen the Adams O2 boiler, they had just off-loaded.**

J. R. G. Griffiths

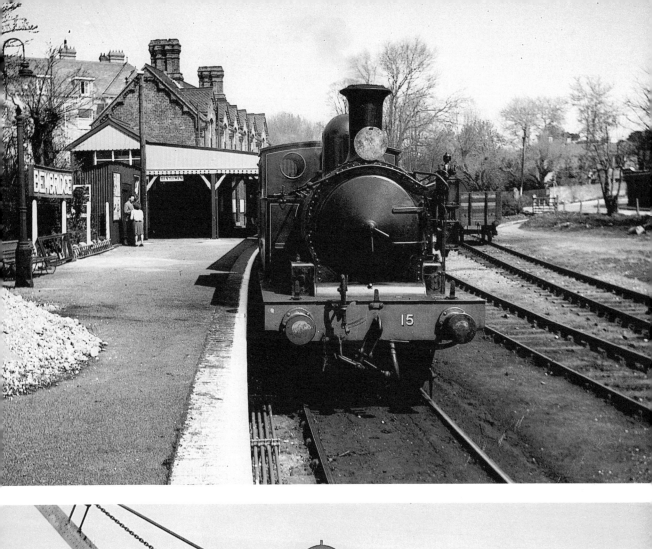

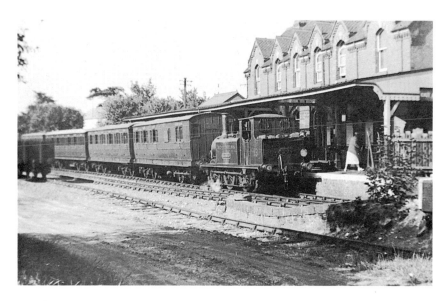

A pre-War photograph of 'Terrier' tank No. 13 *Carisbrooke* shortly after arrival at Bembridge with a train from Brading.
The Peter Joyce Collection

'Terrier' No. 13 *Carisbrooke* backs onto the turntable at Bembridge, prior to running round its train.
The Peter Joyce Collection

Terminus station of this branch line, but it did boast the only turntable on the Island capable of turning locomotives.

BEMBRIDGE

BEMBRIDGE TOLL ROAD - 1933

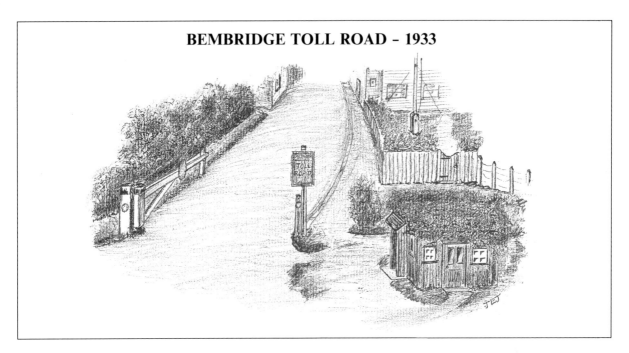

This original toll hut was covered in thick ivy. It was replaced later however, by a much larger one and at this time the toll for a vehicle was 6d and 1d for each pedestrian.

A view of Bembridge station from the buffer blocks beyond the turntable.

J. R. G. Griffiths

Chapter Three – The Newport-Merstone-Sandown Line

BLACKWATER

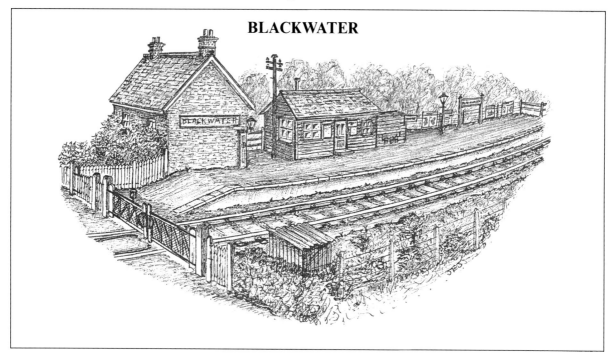

Blackwater was situated in the very centre of the Island and like all village stations had its heyday before the advent of the motor omnibus and the private car.

Situated on the outskirts of Newport, Shide was not a busy station passenger wise, but more for the chalk that was quarried close by, for the manufacture of cement.

SHIDE

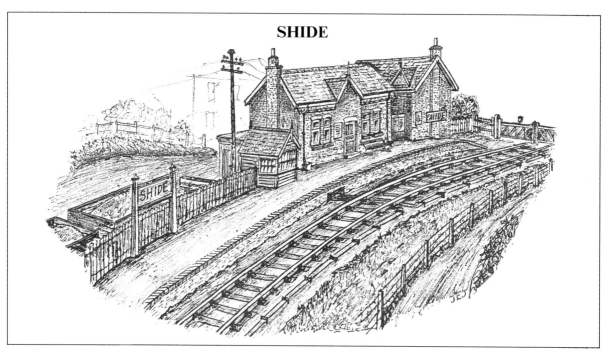

Newport station staff – Saturday 4th May 1946. This photograph was taken outside the staff room at the south end, with an E1 tank locomotive in the background. Back row, left to right: Fred Richardon, Joe Leal and Bill Lowthian, front row: H. Hobbs, Bill Eldridge, Ray Gray and Ern Chapman.

Bill Lowthian

Blackwater station, complete with milk churns on the end of the platform.

J. R. G. Griffiths

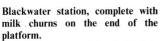

3rd-SINGLE SINGLE-3rd
Horringford to
MERSTONE
(S) 4d H FARE 4d H (S)
For Conditions see over   For Conditions see over
2382

3rd. SINGLE
Alverstone to
NEWCHURCH
(S) 2d H FARE 2d H (S)
FOR CONDITIONS SEE OVER.
2000

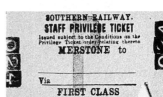

SOUTHERN RAILWAY.
STAFF PRIVILEGE TICKET
Issued subject to the Conditions on the Privilege Ticket order relating thereto
MERSTONE to
Via
FIRST CLASS
024

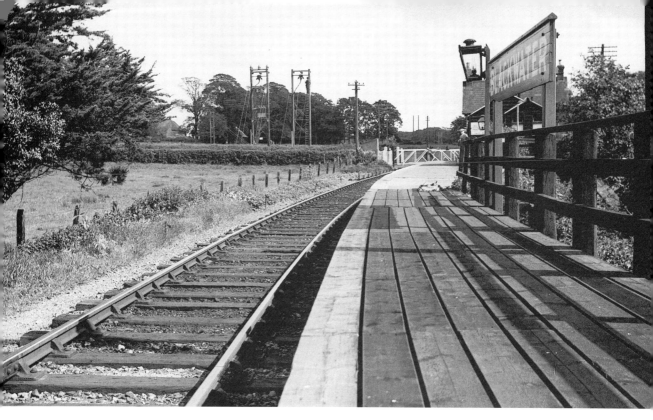

The Southern Railway rebuilt the platform at Blackwater to a length of 242ft. A station house was located adjacent to the level crossing.

J. R. G. Griffiths

Blackwater level crossing gates fresh after repairs and painting following partial demolition by an E1 class tank engine.

J. R. G. Griffiths

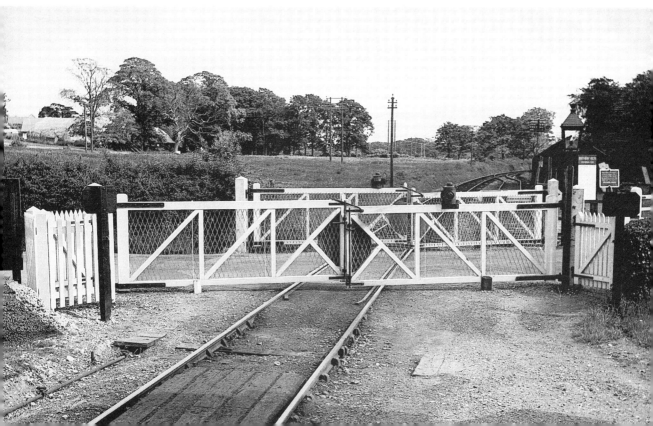

MERSTONE

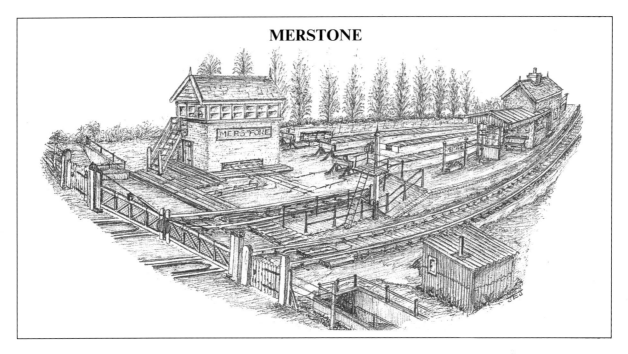

In the centre of the farming community, Merstone was the crossing station of the Newport–Sandown line, and also where passengers changed for the Ventnor West branch line.

The northern end of Merstone station in the mid-1930s, looking towards Newport. On the platform is a stop mark for the guidance of drivers, whilst in the siding is a collection of ex-LCDR four-wheel carriages.

J. R. G. Griffiths

A close-up photograph of the driving end of one of the ex-LBSCR push-pull sets used on the Ventnor West branch. Of particular interest is the unpanelled carriage end which carried electric lights, windscreen wiper and a compressed air whistle. This 57ft 7in long carriage is pictured berthed at Merstone.

J. R. G. Griffiths

Motor train working was a feature of the Ventnor West branch for many years. Pictured at Merstone in 1936 is a brake third coach ex-LCDR four-wheeler No. 4112, with the carriage set number 484 clearly painted on the rear. This particular coach is currently under restoration to full working order at the Isle of Wight Steam Railway, where it will eventually run with one of the Brighton 'Terrier' tanks, thus creating an Island scene of a bygone era.

J. R. G. Griffiths

Another mid-thirties picture of Merstone station, but this view is taken from the signal box. Waiting for the next train is a collection of assorted milk churns which was such a common scene on the Island railways in steam days.

J. R. G. Griffiths

An interesting view of Merstone station taken from by the crossing gates showing the signal box on the left and the distinctive lower quadrant wooden post signals – complete with finials.

J. R. G. Griffiths

A rare, close-up view of the levers of Merstone signal box.

J. R. G. Griffiths

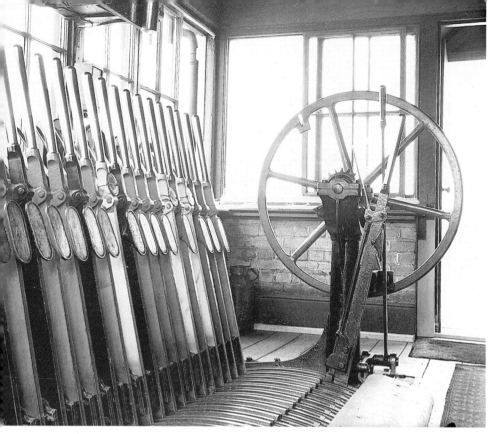

Another interior view of Merstone signal box, showing the lever frame and level crossing wheel.

J. R. G. Griffiths

A picture of the level crossing gates at Merstone taken from the signal box looking towards Sandown. The line on the left went on to Sandown whereas the line on the right veered off towards Ventnor.

J. R. G. Griffiths

The passenger under-path at Merstone station, quite typically flooded.

J. R. G. Griffiths

The sad scene at Merstone station on 27th October 1957, following the closure of the Newport–Sandown line in 1956.

H. P. Mason

HORRINGFORD

A typical rural station, but like all the others it had had its moments of glory. All the local farmers would bring cattle and produce to sell at Newport on market days, and the villagers would enjoy a day in town to purchase their requirements; all in all a busy place in years gone by. In latter years though, a brisk trade was carried on by loading and transporting sugar beet.

Horringford station in 1937 plays host to an industrious team of Island railway staff. Left to right are: Carpenter and cartoonist Jimmy E. James, Bert Vanner, Porter Sam Wells and Charlie Taylor.

J. R. G. Griffiths

NEWCHURCH

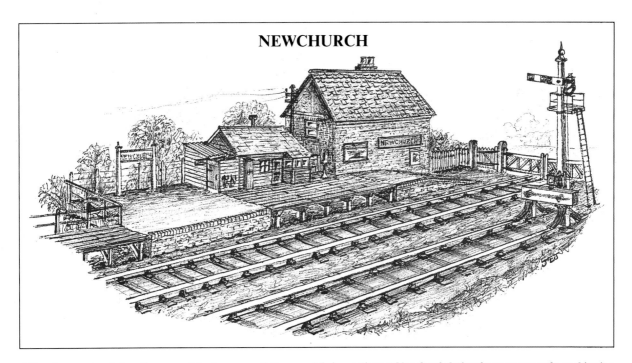

Although a country station, it was surprising how many visitors spent their vacations at Newchurch during the summer months, making it a base for their activities.

Just over a mile from Sandown on the Newport line, Alverstone attracted large numbers of visitors to enjoy boating on a winding stream that ran parallel to the track. This recreation started from a nearby adjoining old mill where teas and refreshments could be obtained, making a very pleasant day out.

ALVERSTONE

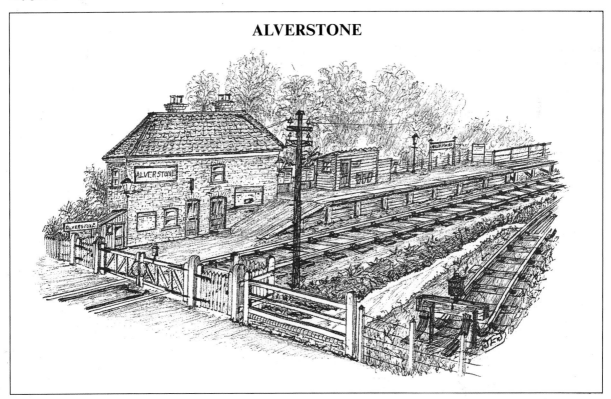

Miss Dorothy F. Whittington

To many Island railway staff and passengers I am known as 'Auntie Dot' the Grade One Porter of Alverstone. My service on the railways was from 17th September 1942 to 11th January 1947, under the watchful eye of Sandown station Master, Mr Attrill. I worked with Dick Russell and some younger boys, Phil Butler and a lad called Goodwin. I used to keep in touch with the station staff at Newchurch and would often send them little parcels via the guards on passing trains.

The duties at Alverstone were interesting and varied and included issuing and collecting tickets, operating the signals, filling the signal lamps and taking them up the posts, cleaning out the station building and so on. During the War there was an anti-aircraft gun at the rear of the station, and the crew who manned it often visited me at the station. The waiting room was warm and we would sit and chat away the time. In those dark days we often had low level bombing raids on Southampton Docks or Cowes boat yards. I remember looking up above the station and seeing the German crews in their aeroplanes quite clearly.

It was hard work in wartime and I basically worked two shifts 6am–1pm and 1pm to 11pm. I had to manage the milk churns on my own – all Newport bound. Whenever I felt like a moan my thoughts turned towards our brave boys fighting the German war machine.

A little stream flowed by alongside the station and I can recall it flooding over on to the railway line on a few occasions. At the very end of my period of service the water froze over completely so that one could stand on it. The winter of 1946/47 was so bad that even the locks of the doors froze! I liked to give the footplate crews a cup of tea when they stopped at the station, in order to warm them up.

In the War years I used to lodge with the 'Young family', and Don Young, one of the children, used to come out to Alverstone station to visit me and do a bit of train spotting. Don is now a well known model railway engineer who builds scale working steam models of Island O2 tank locomotives – and good they are too! He is also editor of the magazine *Locomotives Large & Small* which often has mention of the Islands' locomotives. A relation of the family worked on the Island railways as a driver. By coincidence an unusual incident happened at Alverstone involving Charlie, in that he failed to stop his regular engine, No. 31 *Chale* at the station. I recall that he did however halt at Newchurch, but the poor passengers had to walk back

Miss Dorothy Whittington at work on Alverstone station.
Dorothy F. Whittington

Dorothy Whittington again, better known to passengers and railway staff as 'Auntie Dot'.
Dorothy F. Whittington

to Alverstone, escorted by a railwayman. Poor Charlie was so red-faced the next time I saw him, but it was wartime and Alverstone station was 'blacked-out', so he wasn't to blame.

In view of the blackout, I was very aware of passengers' safety and one day I painted the platform edge white to help them when boarding or detraining. Yes, I had a real pride in my station at Alverstone and I made sure that the roses in the station gardens were looked after. On one occasion I was locked out of the station building, but as luck would have it, Jimmy James the carpenter, had put in a new pane of glass the day before. I simply removed the putty and climbed in through the window. After letting myself in I made good by replacing the glass and no one was the wiser.

I was sad to leave the railway, but the men were now returning to their jobs from National Service and I had done my bit.

Chapter Four – The Ventnor West Branch
(Merstone Junction–Ventnor West)

GODSHILL

Bill Lewis

A well built station but well away from the village itself. Godshill's main attraction of course, is its ancient church and the olde worlde style of its buildings.

I had the opportunity of commencing my railway career at the prettiest station on the Isle of Wight and therefore started in 1945 at Ventnor West. In those days we a had a grade one porter-signalman named Alec Widger working out at Ventnor West. He was actually part-time as half his time was spent at Wroxall and the remaining time with us. When I started at Ventnor West we had a Station Master who was Ron Bennett, the signalman's father. Junior grade railwaymen like me in those days were not allowed to work on Sundays, but Mr Bennett would often approach me unofficially and offer me a pound to work on the Sunday.

The highlight of every week, which station staff looked forward to, was pay day on Thursday. Sometimes I would look at my pay packet when Mr Bennett gave it to me and ask him if I had been overpaid. He would look back at me and smile saying, "You did a couple of hours overtime" or, "It must have been a slip of the pen". Mr Bennett was always very kind and thoughtful to his staff, who thought the world of him. During the War the

booking clerk was Mrs Marjorie Dennis and she would regularly cut Mr Bennett's hair, as she was a hairdresser by trade. One day, whilst having his hair cut in the parcels office at Ventnor West, Mr Bennett was visited by the carpenter, Jimmy James. However, Jimmy was better known for his handy work with a pen and paper. Sure enough, an amusing cartoon sketch of Mr Bennett appeared on the notice board, courtesy of guess who?

It was very much a family service at Ventnor West in those days. The first train of the day was the 8.10am departure, which was a push-pull two-coach train hauled by a Brighton 'Terrier', either No. 8 *Freshwater* or No. 13 *Carisbrooke*. We would walk out onto the platform and check to make sure all our regular passengers were on board the train. In the mornings there would be a goods guard on the train, as a coal truck would be brought down on the first working from Merstone. This coal wagon would then be unloaded by Gubbins & Ball and taken to the hospital for their coal-fired

Godshill station nameboard. This was recently discovered, along with a number of other redundant Island Station nameboards, in use in a former railwayman's garden as a footpath!

J. R. G. Griffiths

boilers. Sometimes there would be as many as six or eight full wagons of coal to be unloaded in the siding at Ventnor West. During the afternoon service, the push-pull trains between Ventnor West and Merstone would be manned by the junior who acted as the ticket seller on the train, as there were no staff at Whitwell, Godshill or St Lawrence halts. Although for two summers after the War Whitwell was manned again by either Sammy Wells, my brother George or myself. The regular drivers on the branch, like Jim Stone or Arthur Turner, taught me to drive the push-pull trains from the carriage end. Many a time I have driven the train from Ventnor West to Merstone in this way.

The winter of 1947 hit Ventnor West particularly harshly and each morning they would send a Brighton 'Terrier' down the line light engine to clear the snow. One morning Driver Monty Harvie was driving engine No. 8 light engine to Ventnor and he noticed a crowd of passengers waiting in arctic conditions at Whitwell station. He took pity on them and stopped the "Little Brighton" and piled them onto the footplate. Somehow, he managed to control No. 8, keeping hold of the regulator and brake, and they crawled into Ventnor West packed like sardines! The passengers really appreciated this highly illegal act which was an incredible sight.

The snow that winter in 1947 was dreadful throughout the Isle of Wight. On our line the snow

Godshill station handled daily milk traffic and the churns on the platform are waiting to be loaded onto the next train to Merstone, where they will be reloaded onto a Newport bound train. The station served the attractive village of Godshill situated approximately half a mile away.

J. R. G. Griffiths

WHITWELL

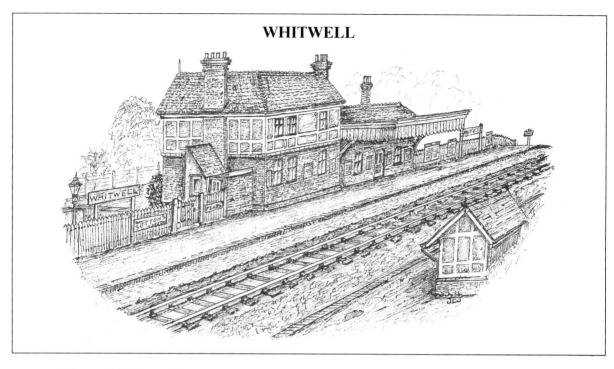

This was originally a crossing station, but when the omnibus took over it was one of the first branch lines to close.

Whitwell station was located on the hillside above the village. The 'up' platform had a main station building containing a booking office, waiting room and station master's house, whilst the 'down' platform only possessed a waiting shelter.

J. R. G. Griffiths

Originally, Whitwell had a passing loop, as pictured on page 83 of *Once Upon a Line ... Volume Two*. However, Southern Railway economies of the 1920s resulted in the lifting of the loop and closure of the signal box.

J. R. G. Griffiths

was blown in the cuttings, causing some deep drifts, which made the train service impossible on occasions. Driver Harold Lacey bravely set out from Merstone one morning on one of the Brighton 'Terrier' tanks only to become buried in the snow before reaching us at Ventnor West. I heard they had to be rescued by another engine of the O2 tank variety, crewed by Driver Teddy Joyce and Fireman Ken West.

As mentioned earlier, the Ventnor West branch was run like a family business. Some of the passengers used to play tricks on us and there was generally high spirits in those far off days. One morning I recall the guard, Bert Foster, sitting waiting in the booking office while his driver waited to depart in the driver's carriage compartment. One of our passengers, Wally Brookman, decided to imitate the guard and shouted to the driver, "Right away, driver". With that the train set off minus their guard. Of course they had to stop and return to the station rather red-faced. Another passenger, Harold Lowe, who boarded the morning train at Whitwell would walk across the field to the Station each morning. If ever Harold was late and the train had to depart without him, the driver would keep an eye open for him until Whitwell station was out of sight. On occasions, they have spotted him running up to the station well after the train had departed and the locomotive and push-pull train has stopped then set back to collect passenger Harold Lowe. This was so typical of the branch and the Isle of Wight railways in those days.

On August Bank Holiday one year we had a derailment at Ventnor West with No. 13 *Carisbrooke*, I believe. Each August there was a flower show at Ventnor Park. It was a particularly hot summer's day and we were expecting extra passengers to visit the show from Godshill, Whitwell and Merstone, so an extra coach was sent down to Ventnor West for the evening return service. The little Brighton 'Terrier' arrived with the extra coach during the afternoon, but when shunting it into the siding beside the station house all six wheels came off the line. I was then sent to Merstone in a taxi with the token in order that a brakedown train from Newport could travel down the branch. Apparently, it was discovered that the derailment was caused by rail buckle as a result of the heat of the day.

Locomotive operation on the branch was of interest in those days as when our regular 'Terrier' tanks Nos 8 *Freshwater* and 13 *Carisbrooke* were absent because of boiler washout or repair, Newport shed would send an O2 tank down to look after the service. This always meant that a guard had to be provided for the late turn of duty to operate the signal box at Ventnor West, as the O2 was not push-pull fitted and therefore had to run around its train. The most unusual engine I ever saw at Ventnor West was the E4 0-6-2 tank No. 2510 which ran during the winter service, between Merstone and Ventnor West for just one week! She ran with just one coach and in my opinion, looked almost as big as the coach. What a sound that engine made as it left the station, but alas I never saw her again.

Sadly, in 1952 I was transferred away from Ventnor West to Wroxall as porter-signalman,

ST LAWRENCE

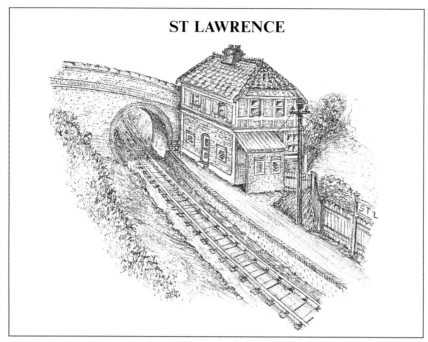

On the outskirts of Ventnor and situated in one of the most picturesque parts of the Island.

St Lawrence station was wedged in between the Downs and a public road and was down-graded to an unstaffed halt from as early as 1927. Noteworthy in this photograph are the delightful advertisements.

J. R. G. Griffiths

Left: **At the end of the 220ft-platform at St Lawrence was a collector's dream – an Isle of Wight Railway Company 'Beware of Trains' metal sign. Today this sign would be worth a small fortune!**
J. R. G. Griffiths

No need for explanation of this lineside sign at Ventnor West.
J. R. G. Griffiths

Originally known as the Town station, but changed to Ventnor West when the Southern took over, it was the terminus of the Merstone branch line.

VENTNOR WEST

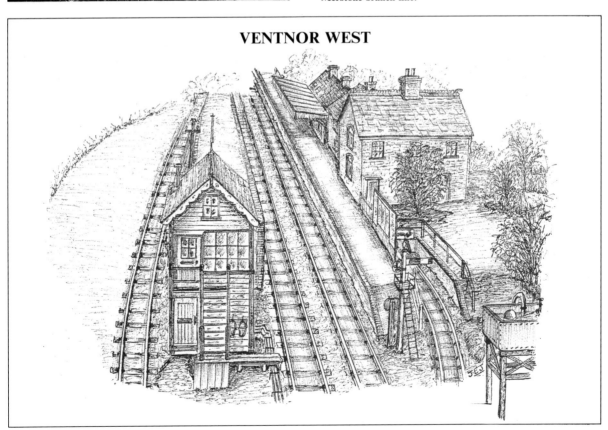

where I succeeded Peter Corad. Here I stayed until leaving the railway service in September 1962. Wroxall station served the small village and was pretty busy in those days. It was at the top of Apse Bank and it was provided with a passing loop, signal box and booking office. The latter was contained in the station building on the 'up' platform. There was just one siding located on the Shanklin side of the station. A tremendous amount of bacon was sent by train from the Flux & Sons bacon factory which was just opposite the siding. Working with me at Wroxall was my father-in-law Arthur Unstead, and Harold Fry who later went to Ventnor.

Part of my duties at Wroxall as porter-signalman was to work at Shanklin and Sandown. One year I was even sent to Ryde St John's Road to help out as a passenger guard.

I will always remember my first few months at Wroxall when learning the job. I walked over the line one morning to collect the single-line staff from the driver of engine No. 22 *Brading*. As I put my hand out to collect the staff I felt that it was covered with oil and grease. Looking up in surprise to the footplate of engine 22 I was greeted by the smiling face of Driver 'Mad' Jack Sturgess. On Jack's return from Ventnor I smeared the staff with paste. The following Sunday No. 22 was booked to work the 11.18am from Ryde to Ventnor, which was an extra train. The return working of this special was booked off Ventnor at 12 o'clock midday, running empty carriage stock – non-stop to Ryde. Now, No. 22 arrived at Wroxall early, before

the service train had pulled into the station from Shanklin. I therefore decided to hold Jack Sturgess's train outside the station on the home signal so that waiting passengers on the 'up' platform would be prevented from boarding this non-stop train by mistake. Next I walked across to the 'down' platform to collect the tickets from passengers off the train arriving from Shanklin. Meanwhile, my colleague Harold Fry, pulled the signals

Push-pull fitted O2 tank No. 35 *Freshwater* draws into Ventnor West with a two-coach set. This locomotive was imported to the Island in 1949 to replace a 'Terrier' tank locomotive which had carried the same name. Note the disc and tail lamp on the engine's buffer beam.
J. R. G. Griffiths

A beautiful view looking towards Merstone, taken from the end of Ventnor West station, showing the signal box and wooden post lower quadrant signals, surrounded by woodland. It has the feeling of an amphitheatre.
J. R. G. Griffiths

and points for *Brading* and her empty carriage stock train to proceed on her way. 'Mad' Jack was obviously expecting me to collect the single-line train staff as, when Harold caught it, he discovered that it was rather hot! Apparently Driver Sturgess had heated the staff whilst waiting outside the station, but poor Harold was not amused.

One year we had a very heavy thunderstorm at Wroxall and I thought the world would end with all the lightning and sound of thunder. Suddenly the instrument exploded in the signal box as did those at Sandown and Shanklin! I knew immediately what had happened, the wires had been struck by a

bolt of lightning. This resulted in pilot working being implemented for some days. In the end the S&T Department imported some instruments to the Island from the Fawley branch near Southampton.

Apse Bank was a gruelling gradient to test the little O2 tank engines, and they had to storm up the 1 in 70 bank from Shanklin to Wroxall. One morning an engine did succumb, when engine 31 *Chale*, driven by Maurie Prouten, blew a piston through the casing. She was in a terrible state and could not reverse back to Shanklin. A light engine was then sent for from St John's Road shed to push

The RCTS special pictured ready for departure from Ventnor West. On the footplate of No. 32 *Bonchurch*, Driver Arthur Turner and Fireman Ken Simmonds show enthusiasts the various controls, while Guard George Pocock has opened the signal box to show his passengers the lever frame.

J. R. G. Griffiths

Driver Arthur Turner stands at ground level next to his engine, No. 32 *Bonchurch* and chats to Mr W. A. Camwell, the well-known photographer and editor of the SLS Journal, while peering down from the footplate is Fireman Ken Simmonds.

J. R. G. Griffiths

Pictured at Ventnor West station are, left to right: Guard Reg Seaman, Bill Lewis and Fireman John 'Oxo' Chambers.

Bill Lewis

Left, is Permanent Way Ganger George Sibbeck, and right, is Bill Lewis, complete with single-line staff under his arm, pictured at Wroxall station.

Bill Lewis

the whole train up to Wroxall. Old *Chale* was then dumped in the 'up' siding before being towed back to Ryde Works for repair.

During the winter timetable one year I recall encountering some difficulty with my neighbouring signal box at Shanklin. Some considerable time after a train should have cleared the Wroxall–Shanklin section the instrument had not cleared. I therefore decided to telephone Signalman Len Langbourne in Shanklin box to find out what the problem was. Len explained to me that the machine would not accept the single-line token. He then discovered that this token was for the

Shanklin–Sandown section. Apparently, whilst chatting with the driver of the Ryde bound train, Len had handed to him the same token as had been surrendered. This situation was quickly remedied as the next 'down' train from Sandown was sent up without a token for the Sandown–Shanklin section, but with the missing Shanklin–Wroxall token. Everything went according to plan and nothing was ever said. This once again shows how everyone on the Island railways helped each other out in those days – if only it were the same today.

Standing in front of 'Terrier' tank No. 8 *Freshwater* at Ventnor West station are, left to right: Fireman Les Fryer, Bill Lewis and Driver Tom Hayward.

Bill Lewis

No. 35 *Freshwater* has just arrived at Ventnor West with the two-coach push-pull set from Merstone. The locomotive's push-pull apparatus can be clearly seen located behind the white disc, below the Westinghouse brake pump.

John A. Britton

The end of the line at Ventnor West, showing the points to the run-round loop.

J. R. G. Griffiths

Chapter Five – The Ryde-Newport-Cowes Line

Hughie V. 'Bill' White

I started off as a carriage cleaner at Ryde Pier and then, after two years, I was offered a job as a porter at Ryde Pier Head. Not long after this I was transferred two stations down the line to Ryde St John's Road as a porter and then eventually to Haven Street as a porter-signalman. In order to take up the vacancy at Haven Street I had to learn all the various rules and regulations and my tutor was Jim Hooper from Newport. My big problem was in learning bell codes and so I wrote them all down on small cards and revised at home, resulting in me passing out in 'flying colours', with top marks.

It was an interesting job out at Haven Street in those days with a shift from 8am until 3pm, with a signalling requirement from 11am until 1.30pm in the box. When Signalman Jess Wheeler transferred to Brading signal box I took over his position as full time signalman at Haven Street. My job as porter-signalman was taken over by a young man called, James. Our immediate boss was Mr Smith, the Station Master at Newport, who was also responsible for the stations at Cowes and Mill Hill.

An unusual part of my duties as porter-signalman at Haven Street was to travel to Newport station and note down every wagon number in the yard, together with their advice notes. If a wagon remained loaded after a given period, the load's owners, like Corrall's or Honor & Geoffrey of Freshwater, would have to make an extra rental payment. This was mostly coal wagon traffic, but

A scene so typical of the Island railways during the steam era, with an O2 tank heading a four-coach set through the Vectis countryside.

J. R. G. Griffiths

in the season there were also sugar beet wagons. Very seldom did one of these private firms leave a wagon loaded for any length of time, but British Railways had to make sure they had their 'pound of flesh' in those days.

Haven Street was a delightful little country station in those days, which was principally a passing loop on the single line between Smallbrook Junction (in the summer months) and Newport, whilst during the Winter Timetable this section was lengthened to Ryde-St Johns with the lines from Smallbrook Junction, running as two independent lines into Ryde. Like many Island stations Haven Street was oil lit right up until closure. It was a lovely station to work at and even sleep at! Yes, on a number of occasions Terry Wright and myself were forced to sleep at the station when there were heavy snow falls. We had a couple of wooden chairs to sleep in and Terry would build the fire right up. However the cold frost would creep up through our 16-lever signalling frame, but you had to be there for duty as the mail train was due to pass in the early hours.

During the summer months a common occurrence between Haven Street and Smallbrook were farm animals straying on to the line. Quite often this would disrupt the passenger service considerably. Towards the end of the steam era the service would also be disrupted by engine failures. I recall that on one occasion Driver Frankie Ash had experienced problems in getting his engine to steam properly because of bad coal supply, in the form of bricketts. I believe he had one of Ryde shed's spare engines, possibly No. 32 *Bonchurch*, at the head of his Cowes bound train, as his regular locomotive was in for boiler washout. Shortly after passing Smallbrook Junction the 'old girl' ran short of

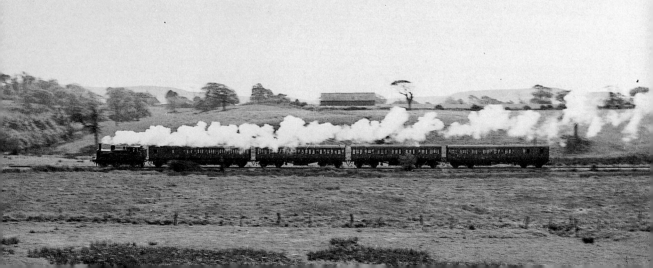

ASHEY

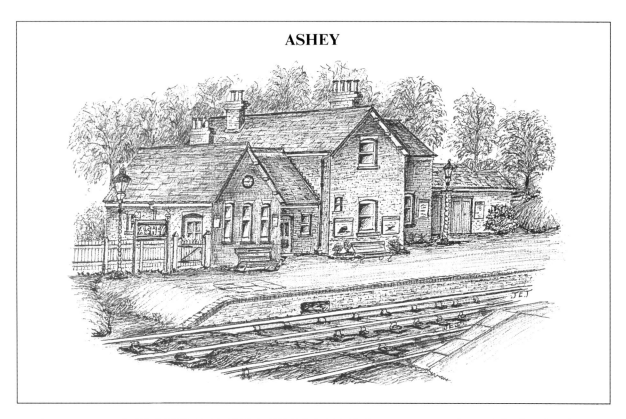

A very isolated station; the reason for its existence may have been the fact that many years ago chalk was quarried from the nearby Downs, for which a spur track was laid to freight the chalk to the station. Another reason may have been the annual race meeting held close to the station. When the racing was abandoned and chalk was no longer quarried the station saw very few passengers.

The temporary station staff of Ashey on 30th March 1959. This was the last occasion that Ashey station was manned for the Ashey race meetings. Several special trains conveying race-goers were laid on for the meeting and extra staff were allocated to the station from Newport and Ryde. Left to right are: Les Allen, who was normally Station Foreman at Ryde St John's Road, Relief Signalman Len Yarney from Newport and Harry Hobbs, a Newport based goods guard. The results of the races were despatched via the single-line token leather pouch to Smallbrook and Havenstreet, where they were relayed to interested railway staff!

J. R. G. Griffiths

HAVEN STREET

Crossing station on the old IWC Newport to Ryde line; in latter years however, it found itself situated on a main bus route. It has survived through to become the headquarters of the Isle of Wight Steam Railway.

Haven Street station looking towards Newport on 4th October 1965. Signalman Terry Wright's motorcycle is parked in front of the station building on the right-hand side of the photograph.

John Goss

At Haven Street Porter Signalman Hughie White collects the single-line token from Driver Cyril Eason on the approaching O2 tank, No. 31 *Chale* which is hauling a Cowes bound train. The crew of No. 33 *Bembridge* look on patiently from the footplate of their locomotive on 10th July 1965.

Tony Scarsbrook

Former Haven Street Porter-Signalman Hughie 'Bill' White starts Ryde Pier tram No. 2 on its way from Ryde Pier Head to Ryde Esplanade on 31st December 1966.

G. S. Cocks

steam and came to a halt by Ashey. An assisting engine then propelled the whole train into Haven Street. The engine assisting at the rear then ran around the train and hauled the failed locomotive and carriages onto Newport.

At nights we quite often had bank fires at Haven Street caused by drivers allowing their firemen to throw out the fire before returning to Ryde St John's Road shed. This would save them time back at the shed and they could get home quicker. Over the years this ash accumulated. The embankment by the distant signal eventually attracted adders that would delight in slithering in the ash. For me a trip up to the distant signal to replace an oil lamp was therefore a hazardous journey! My colleague Terry Wright on the other hand, had no such fear of snakes, having lived for a period of time in Australia where snakes are more common. Terry designed and constructed a device with a wire loop at the end for catching adders. He caught many snakes like this and left them dead on the wire fence at the back of Haven Street box. In fact one of the biggest frights I ever had at Haven Street station was to be confronted face to face with an adder

wriggling out of the coal bunker into the toilets. On this occasion I had no other choice but to put Terry's snake catching device into use. Thinking back I realise why the snake was heading for the toilet. Snakes like water and I had left the toilet tap on for two days prior to this, in order to thoroughly clean out the urinal. I often sit back and wonder if the preservationists who now run the Isle of Wight Steam Railway have encountered any adders at Haven Street.

Following the closure of the Ryde–Newport–Cowes line in February 1966 my own station at Haven Street closed to passenger traffic. I well remember pulling the levers for that final passenger train, hauled by engine 14 *Fishbourne* with Driver Ken West at the regulator. The line continued to remain in use between Smallbrook Junction and Medina Wharf for freight traffic, but Haven Street's points were set for through working only and the station building was boarded up.

Situated in a deep cutting and far from village activities it was one of the first stations to find bus opposition too strong. It was also subject to minor landslides and delays to traffic were quite frequent.

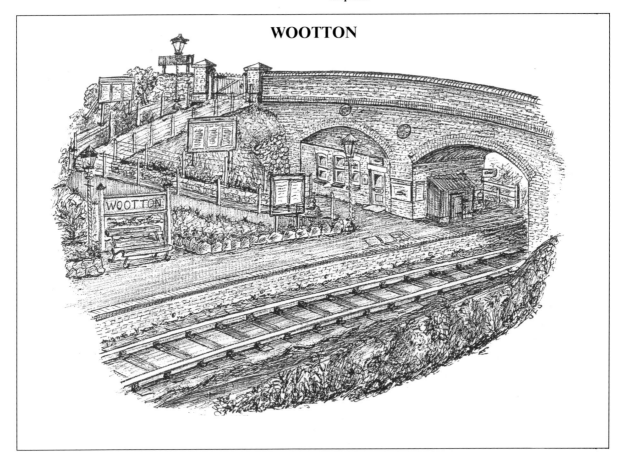

WOOTTON

Wootton station, facing towards Haven Street, showing the booking office and waiting room located beneath the arch of the bridge.

J. R. G. Griffiths

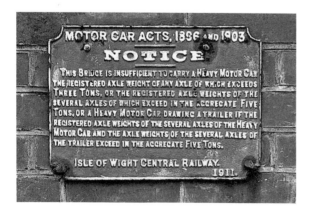

This unusual notice was located on the bridge over the railway line at Wootton station and was still in place until the 1970s. The photographer took this picture of the IWCR notice on 10th July 1965.

Tony Scarsbrook

The station seat at Wootton station has clearly printed, 'Wootton for Woodside'. One wonders if the new station at Wootton, built by the Isle of Wight Steam Railway, will also have similarly inscribed station seats?

J. R. G. Griffiths

FISHBOURNE FERRY TERMINAL – 1950

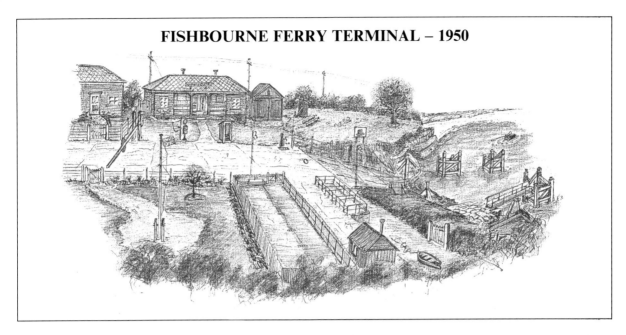

At this time cattle as well as cars used the ferries, as the pens and enclosures depict. Of course, the ships were a lot smaller, as was the staff, but it is notable that the Station Master lived on the premises.

My next move was a transfer to Smithard's Lane crossing which was situated between Medina Wharf and Mill Hill station on the outskirts of Cowes. My assignment was to look after the crossing gates as crossing keeper. I never once had to open the gates for a train to pass, but a legal technicality of a local by-law prevented the crossing from being unmanned. For six months or so I just sat there reading books, magazines and newspapers, and watched the weeds grow. This was a very depressing task for a railwayman who enjoyed watching and working with trains. Finally, after Smithard's Lane crossing was closed permanently I transferred back to Ryde Pier as a tram driver. Once again closure followed me as I was the last person to drive a tram down the pier, in January 1969.

On summer Saturdays we used to do twelve trips an hour between Ryde Esplanade and Ryde Pier Head. The trams were limited to 88 people officially, but I have known them packed with standing room only! That's how I always wish to remember the Island railways, busy and flourishing.

An interesting view, looking from Whippingham station towards Wootton. As can be seen, there was quite a gradient to test locomotives and drivers, with a climb of 1 in 64 up Whippingham Bank.

J. R. G. Griffiths

WHIPPINGHAM

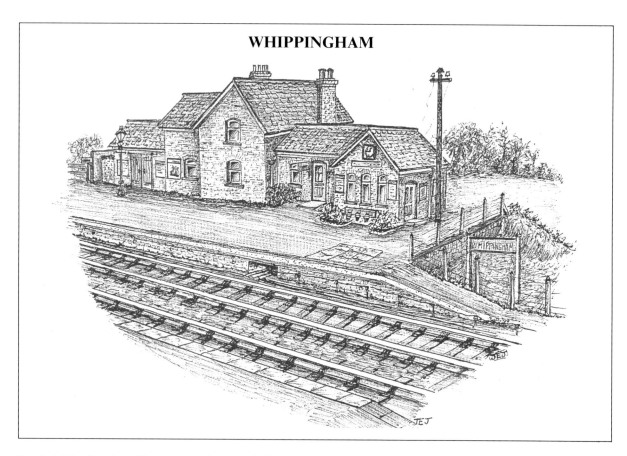

Very isolated and rarely used by passengers; the reason for its existence at all must be because of its close proximity to Osborne House which enabled Queen Victoria to take advantage of it when she visited the Island.

O2 class No. 23 *Totland* descends the 1:64 incline from Wootton into Whippingham station with a train bound for Newport and Cowes. The station and garden look particularly well maintained with whitewashed edging stones.

J. R. G. Griffiths

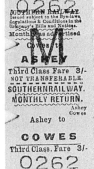

The station sign at Whippingham on the 'down' platform. The station closed in September 1953 but the crossing loop remained in use until 1956 according to the Island railway staff.

J. R. G. Griffiths

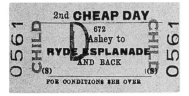

Marjorie Smith

My father, George Henry Edwards, was a Station Master at three of the Isle of Wight Central stations between 1906 and 1926. He started at Haven Street which, in those days, was just a simple structure on the north side of the line with a siding into the small gasworks opposite. In my father's time at Haven Street there was no passing loop as trains passed at Ashey, the next station down the line towards Ryde.

In 1910 we moved to Wootton, the next station down the line towards Newport. In those days the station was always announced, "Wootton for Woodside" when trains arrived in the platform. It was a strange set up at Wootton with the booking office located beneath the arch of the road bridge at the Haven Street end of the platform. We lived in the Station Master's house which was built a few years before we moved in.

Seven years later, our family moved again to

Whippingham station which was again just one station down the line towards Newport, and Dolly Morey who later married Bill Miller the driver, took over the running of Wootton station. Whippingham had a passing loop in those days and was quite busy. It is probably better known as the station which served the Royal Estate at Osborne. The only royal visitor we ever saw however was young Louis Mountbatten, who used the station to get to the Naval Cadet College. He was a dashing boy in those days, so smart and well spoken. Lord Mountbatten as he later became, always used the service trains and was just like an ordinary passenger.

Every evening I would help my father light the paraffin oil lamps along the platform. Sometimes my brother, who was a relief station master, would be sent to look after our station, until he transferred to the mainland in 1925. I remember one evening watching a dog fox and vixen trot along the platform and across the line – "A true country

A view taken from platform level, looking along the 'up' side of Whippingham station, towards Wootton.

J. R. G. Griffiths

The view from the middle of the foot crossing at Whippingham, looking towards Newport. On the right are the station buildings and station master's house with the 'up' platform for Ryde bound trains. By contrast the 'down' platform on the left contains only a small waiting room.

J. R. G. Griffiths

NEWPORT DRAWBRIDGE AND SOUTH SIGNAL BOX

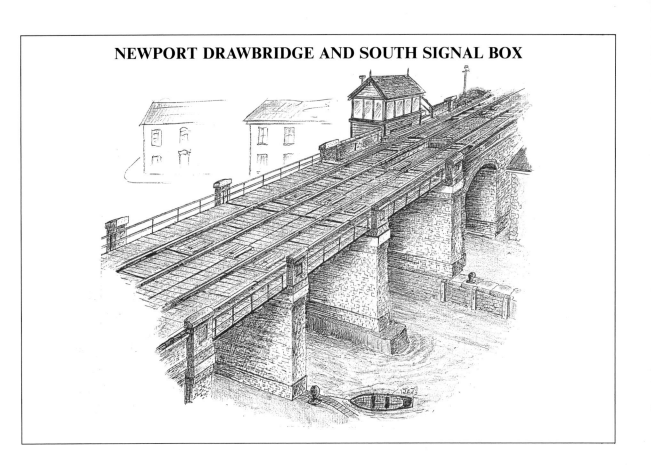

Headquarters of the old Isle of Wight Central Railway Company and up to 1965, one of the biggest employers of labour in the town.

NEWPORT

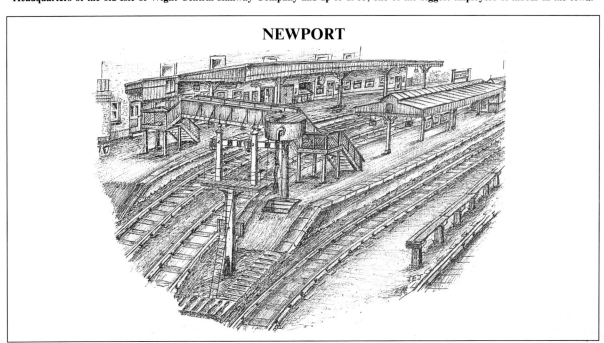

Signalman George Abbott collects the single-line token from Fireman John Farrington on No. 24 *Calbourne*, whilst Driver Tony Tiltman applies 24's Westinghouse brake. Meanwhile, on the 'up' platform, No. 29 *Alverstone* prepares to depart from Newport station with a train for Ryde. As can be seen from the puddles on the platform a cloud has just burst, providing train crews with a wet slippery rail – just right for losing your feet!

Mike Esau

Driver Arthur Turner waits to depart from Newport aboard his O2 tank No. 32 *Bonchurch*, with the RCTS special of May 1952. Engine 32 glistens in the sunlight – a credit to the hard work and spit and polish of Fireman Ken Simmonds.

J. R. G. Griffiths

The lady in this picture was photographed at Newport station on the day of the LCGB "Vectis Farewell" rail tour on Sunday, 3rd October 1965. She was a most interesting lady by the name of Hannah Elizabeth Winter and lived next to the railway line in one of the terraced cottages opposite the station at Haven Street. The name of her cottage was 'Fairview' and following her death the cottage was loaned to the Isle of Wight Steam Railway. Her house was used for a temporary museum of Island railway relics and committee room for society meetings.

Miss Winter was a warm and friendly lady who related many a railway anecdote to railway enthusiasts. She frequently told of her experiences of being on the 'last trains' on the Island branches, and was often given unofficial footplate rides by railway staff. Indeed, when the redundant stock was moved from Ryde to Newport in 1967, the steam-hauled train paused at Haven Street to collect Miss Winter. She was truly an Isle of Wight railway character who will be remembered by all Island railway enthusiasts as one of the main supporters of the railway system – a legend in her own time.

Pictured behind Miss Winter is Driver Ken West climbing aboard engine No. 24 *Calbourne*, whilst on the platform Newport station foreman, Arthur Day waits to give Miss Winter some red carpet treatment.

G. S. Cocks

Women were employed to clean out the compartments and polish the brass handles, whilst the men would wash the outside of the coaches. When the train was in the siding the electric lighting fitters would check the batteries, and renew any faulty bulbs.

station, Whippingham", was my thought at the time.

In theory trains were given the 'right of way' in preference to boat traffic on the Whippingham–Newport section. However, Signalman Ernie Landon would as often as not allow a boat to pass under the railway and open the Medina drawbridge at Newport even though he knew that a service train was due. This used to make my father very cross and I can tell you that there have been many heated conversations between Whippingham

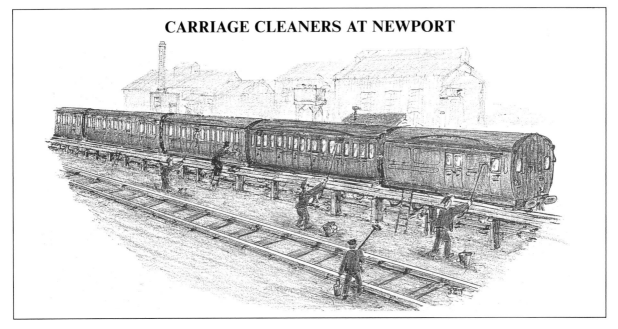

CARRIAGE CLEANERS AT NEWPORT

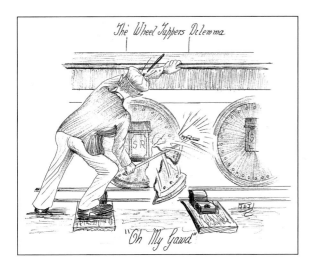

The Wheel Tappers Dilemma

"Oh My Gawd"

"Sorry Arthur"

Foreman Coach Painter 'Arthur Harris,'
trying to keep to the straight & narrow
in the Newport Paint Shop.

LIGHTEN OUR DARKNESS

RINSO

FOR USE IN EMERGENCY

Carriage Electrician at Newport for many years.
— from Tewkesbury —

station and Newport 'A' signal box in bygone years!

In later years in life I maintained contact with the Island railways by marrying porter-signalman Reg Smith of Brading, and I continued to keep in touch with my old friends for some years.

W. G. 'Bill' Dumper

My association with the Isle of Wight railways lasted just seven years, and many times I've wished I'd gone across very much earlier – to have been part of the system when it flourished, before the shadows of closure lengthened.

Some cuts had already been made before I arrived – the previous lot in 1954 – but life was very far from depressing at first. I was 47, and had been around a good deal in the clerical service when I applied for the post of Chief Clerk to the Assistant for Isle of Wight at Newport, in succession to a legend of a man – sadly crippled – named Edgar Charles Prismall, known always as 'Sam'.

I didn't think I was a good interviewee, but apparently my two benign inquisitions at Woking thought I'd 'do'. Accordingly, soon after seven on the bitter morning of Monday, 28th January 1963, I set off from my home station at Exmouth, landing up at Newport, via Salisbury, Portsmouth and Ryde, around about one o'clock.

Up the old iron staircase to 'Newport Office', where I was to spend the three happiest years of my railway life. My chief was to prove a most complex character – G. H. R. Gardener. He was at lunch when I arrived, so I was immediately taken under the wing of Miss Hilda ('Topsy') Evans. This was a redoubtable staff clerk who had spent most of her time on the Island or at Portsmouth, and she taught me so much about my new berth in half-an-hour or so. To describe each new colleague as 'a character' would be boring, but that's exactly what they were. It was the most charismatic place, as we'd say nowadays. I'd even encountered Sam Prismall who was on retirement leave, so he didn't actually hand over to me – but a few days earlier he and I had conducted a shrieked conversation over railway telephone lines. I'd caught about one word in ten, but he had a slightly better average, I believe! Anyway, I'd gathered that there were four other office staff beside himself, and he noted my appeal for help with digs.

The four others immediately fed me information about the job, and the extraordinary thing was that

The morning conference. The Assistant for the Isle of Wight Railways, George H. R. Gardener, discusses the day's business with his faithful servant W. G. 'Bill' Dumper.
Network SouthEast

The behind-the-scenes heroes of the Island railways. Pictured left to right are: Ron Russell, W. G. 'Bill' Dumper, Joan Pritchard, Jack Collard, Janice Lakin, George H. R. Gardener and Charlie Bishop.
Network SouthEast

they all seemed pleased to see me. Not always one's experience when taking up a new job! There was Jan, our telephone operator/girl Friday, petite and full of life, daughter of the previous permanent way inspector, there was Margaret Cole, as she then was, from Chale Green, who later married Brian White, at that time booking clerk at Newport. Margaret liked and understood people; she was a first-class colleague and quite the best girl clerk I've ever worked with. Topsy, like many 'challenging' women, could be quite feminine at times. She talked a lot in parables, "Ah, there's a story attached to that, Bill," she'd say, if I asked her

something, and that story would really make the facts stick in one's mind. Then there was Roy Ingleton, slim, quiet, with a dry humour. Roy had taken over as trains clerk not long before from another 'institution' – Ted Wheeler. Roy was a distance runner of some note, and on the evenings he decided to run home to Ryde after work, he could tidy up, change, and set off with the same organised efficiency as he plotted out passing times and carriage-cleaning visits.

Finally, occupying the only non-clerical desk and chair was Area Inspector Ron Russell, full of experience and fun, always helpful, with just the

right pitched voice to go with his laconic remarks. Yes, you could well understand his "Spector Russell" being mistaken by the chap on the line for "Rowlands Castle"! Ron kindly escorted me later that day to Brading, to the home of Mr and Mrs Reginald Smith. Marjorie, a signalman's wife and from a railway family herself, was a super cook and a wonderful friend. The digs were fantastic, as many Relief Station Masters and others who'd stayed there would agree – Edgar King, Bert Cutler, loads of them. Marjorie told me all about the old days. She had a brother who had once been Station Master at Whippingham, and I remember her describing the life and high jinks which went on in the refreshment room at Newport on a Saturday evening. Of course, the place had closed down long before I went there, but we did use it as an overflow for parcels when we opened the depot in September 1966. A sad comedown, indeed.

Back to my first afternoon at Newport, when I met 'my most unforgettable railway character'. George Gardener 'explained the Island' to me in two concentrated, quick-fire sessions – geography, history, people, installations. He was the fastest talker I ever met, and you had to be on the ball to follow his reasoning, to remember what he'd said, to understand at times the actual subject of his remarks, often produced with little introduction! He once explained a complicated staffing situation to Tony Lamb, then, I believe, at Medina Wharf. He talked at length, finished abruptly and said something like, "Well, there you are. Don't suppose you understood it. Now Mr Dumper'll go over it again." And away he went.

He was impatient, remembered everything, pretended to be tough but was really sentimental, loved the arts and his Wimbledon, had had the job for a quarter of a century, and never, as far as any of us knew, did any harm to anybody. Just the man to run what was like a family – keeping in daily touch with everybody, organising retirement parties and 'do's' of all kinds. Like most of us, he hated his name to be mis-spelt, "He calls me GAR-DYE-NER," he would say, looking carefully at an offending letter 'I' in the middle of his name, replacing the correct 'E'. We had a farewell lunch together in London before I retired to Cornwall. We'd always exchanged Christmas cards, but after the first year or so down here, George's card came no more. An unusual personality whom it had been a privilege to know.

My job, involving correspondence concerned with all the departments, was the most interesting in a varied career. After the old office 'folded' I set up the parcels depot at Newport – interesting, exhausting at first, but not like the job I went there to do in the first place. Incidentally, perhaps something of a record, I applied for the same job three times. I applied for the job as a permanent one, then, when I'd done it for some time, they re-advertised it as temporary, then later on advertised yet again on a permanent basis. Pleased to say I was successful each time!

In my too-short stay on the Island there were plenty of laughs and some sadness. Ken, in the stores, died tragically young. A mention of just a few of the very friendly crowd. There were some very sound, rather more serious men, Ray Draper and Eddie Spears, and Ron Bennett; my two 'older brothers', S. M. Bert Smith and Loco Foreman Bob Menzies, always ready to help and advise when G. H. R. G. was away; the lads who loved a chuckle, like Des Boynton and John Veale, and the large and even-genial C&W Foreman Ern Cox; Ern O'Dell and all the first aiders; all the LDC men, including Driver Nelson Parsons, supposedly a 'fire-eater'. In fact, a most reasonable chap who loved his job and was a very good friend; Dr John Mackett, who would pop in occasionally for a chat about some point of railway history of particular interest to him at the time.

A greatly changed Newport now. Where are the Parsleys, who used to live in the station flat, I wonder? Good old days, and I'm happy to have a reminder of them each Christmas with a card and a little note from good friends Mrs Marjorie Smith at Bedhampton and Brian and Margaret White at Cowes.

W. G. Dumper:	
Newport Office	Jan. 1963–Feb. 1966.
Newport Parcels (New Depot)	July 1966–May 1967.
Special Duties (I.W. Traffic)	May 1967–June 1968.
Newport Parcels	June 1968–Dec. 1969.

Driver Jack Bradford eases No. 20 *Shanklin* over the points at Newport station on 7th August 1965. The second vehicle in the train is of particular interest as it is the former LBSCR saloon carriage which had been converted to a departmental breakdown carriage.

Tony Scarsbrook

Cyril Henley

After leaving the Army at the end of the Second World War I applied for a job on the Island railways in 1946. In those days it wasn't 'what you knew, it was who you knew', and Walt Lee from Bembridge put a good word in for me. As a result I was offered a job in the Signalling & Telegraph Department working for Mr W. A. Barton, whose reminiscences are told in *Once Upon a Line... Volume Two*.

My first assignment was to assist with the renewal of the wiring from 40lb iron to 200lb copper. Promotion was swift and I soon took over as supervisor of the gang. When this task was completed, I was then given the job of looking after

communications and treadles, as well as general signalling maintenance, based at Newport.

One of the first problems I was sent out to cure was at Pound Crossing on the Newport–Freshwater line. The lady crossing keeper had reported to Bill Barton that the warning bells indicating the approach of a train were failing. To begin with I examined the treadle which the locomotives passed over and sent a pulse to sound the bell back at Pound Crossing. This appeared to be in first class condition. Next I examined the bells, but these appeared to be fine. I then looked at the electrical coil and discovered a nest of mice who had eaten the insulation, causing some shorting. Another problem caused by local wildlife was a regular call out at Smallbrook Junction. Here, blue tits would break into the test case and build their nests. Shrews were another recurring problem. They would bite through the wires and one would find their remains after they had been electrocuted.

After the closure of the Freshwater, Ventnor West and Bembridge branches, we were given

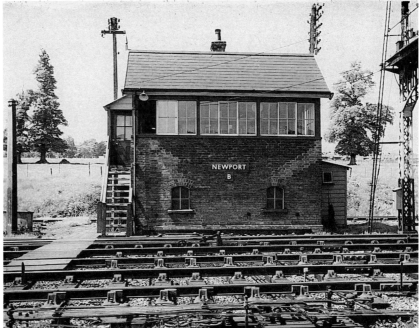

Driver Harry 'Toby' Watson drifts into Newport station on E1 tank No. 3 *Ryde* which is hauling the evening freight from Medina Wharf on 10th May 1958.

H. P. Mason

Newport 'B' signal box, or Newport North as it was formerly known, was a 36-lever frame box. Until the installation of the ex-Waterloo Junction signal box at Ryde St John's Road by the Southern Railway, this signal box at Newport was the largest on the Island. With the closure of Newport 'A' (South Box) in 1958, the remaining signalling at that end was connected up to the North Box. The photograph shows the complexity of the 'lead away' as the point rods and signal wires leave the box. A noteworthy point is the electric light on the fascia board, which was provided to illuminate the token exchanges with passing trains in front of the box, during hours of darkness.

J. R. G. Griffiths

additional responsibilities of looking after points throughout the Island and the telephone exchanges at Newport station and Yarmouth Slipway. This meant we were always hard at work and even on rest days were called out to 'run the token' at various signal boxes. By this, I mean that on summer Saturdays, when it was very busy, I would be sent out to Sandown signal box where I would assist the signalman. The single-line token would be passed up and down on a hoist to the box which was elevated above the station canopy. I would then collect or deliver the token to passing trains.

Just before the summer service commenced each year, we would travel all around the Island railway network and wash out the batteries and give them a good overhaul. We would start off at Ventnor and work up to Ryde, then progress towards Cowes,

This photograph shows one of the former Isle of Wight Central Railway water carrying wagons at Newport goods yard. At this time wagon No. 428S was in use as part of a weed killing train and is seen stabled in between two ex-LSWR road vans.

J. R. G. Griffiths

Three ex-Isle of Wight Railway 12-ton open wagons were transferred to the Locomotive Running Department for use at Newport shed. They are seen in this picture stabled alongside the coaling stage outside the shed.

J. R. G. Griffiths

followed by Newport to Freshwater and the remainder of the network. Just two of us, Harold Sheath and myself, would service every battery on the 60-mile Island railway system.

The locomotive crews were always very obliging in steam days as they would stop their trains on Lake Road bridge and allow me to get off the train to return home. It could be said that I had my own private railway station, I guess. Now I have retired,

Signalman Jim Hooper has just handed the single-line token for the Newport–Cowes section to the driver of the approaching Cowes bound train. He can be seen with his back to the locomotive, about to walk up the steps of Newport 'B' Signal box.
J. R. G. Griffiths

British Rail have constructed a new halt at Lake – little did they know trains had been stopping there since 1946 at least twice a day!

An unusual panoramic view of Medina Wharf taken from an overhead crane gantry showing an E1 tank locomotive hard at work shunting heavy coal trucks.
Larry Watson Collection

Jimmy E. James

A great deal of publicity has been given to train drivers – firemen – guards – signalmen – porters and p.w. staff, granted a very important part of a railway system, perhaps one may even say, 'the Elite'. But in fact there were many more railway servants, all necessary cogs in a great machine, without which even the Elite could not operate.

One particular section that comes to mind are the lonely crossing gate keepers, all over the system and in the most outlandish places, they had to rise very early in the morning, and in all weathers, for mail trains, and were often called upon very late at night.

In the heyday of the glamorous days of steam their cottages were lit by oil lamps, they used water drawn from wells or delivered daily in containers, and used coal for heating, they were very often so isolated that it was an event to receive a visitor.

There were such places in the Island system; Mrs Prouter at Watchingwell for instance, a station rarely visited but when the occasion arose there was always tea and cakes soon after arrival.

Mrs Bennett at Smithards Lane crossing (Cowes) was of the same generous nature, as was

The view looking towards Cowes in March 1966, showing Smithards Lane Crossing 'down' home signal and the Gas House siding.
Timothy P. Cooper

Fireman Tony Toogood looks out of the cab of No. 28 *Ashey* with a train bound for Ryde on 6th January 1964. Driver Peter Mills has opened the regulator and is accelerating just south of Gas House siding.
Timothy P. Cooper

Smithards Lane Crossing in 1965, with the gates closed ready for an approaching train.

Timothy P. Cooper

Mrs Western of Ean crossing (Whitwell) and if we visited Carisbrooke there was Mrs Pile all ready with tea and a good natter.

Mrs Trench at Pound crossing (Calbourne) was always pleased to see us, and I recall an occasion there when I was told to go and milk the goat tethered in the garden whilst the kettle was boiling!

There were others whose names I regret I cannot remember, but they were all essential to the running of a successful Railway.

Mrs Elizabeth Bennett

Just after the Second World War broke out, I started work at Smithards Lane level crossing just outside Mill Hill on the Newport side. In those days the crossing cottage was lived in by Miss Dew who was the full time crossing keeper at Smithards Lane. The name Smithards Lane actually originates from the words, 'Smithy's Lane' as there was a smithy's workshop located nearby. The level crossing was opened about 1890 at about the time

when that area of Cowes was being built up on account of housing for the shipyard workers. The level crossing was located on a steep hill and the gates were unusual in that the upper gate opened across the line, and the lower one further down the slope.

The crossing was widely used by pedestrians, but vehicles rarely crossed as the motorists found it more convenient to reach Newport Road via Artic Road. The operation of the level crossing was quite straightforward. In the case of 'down' trains, a treadle arrangement in the track located some distance to the south activated a bell at the crossing when an approaching train passed over it. Once the bell had sounded, I would pull the lever locking the pedestrian gates, open the gates and pull off the signal for the train to pass. With trains travelling in the 'up' direction from Cowes to Newport and Ryde, we had an earlier advance warning, as a bell in Cowes signal box was rung as the train left the station. This warning bell sounded both at Mill Hill station and at Smithards Lane level crossing. Mention of the signals, reminds me that both stop signals were the standard SR rail-built upper quadrant type, but they were not protected by distant yellow-arm signals as is usual railway practice.

During the War, one really felt in the front line

The lever frame at Smithards Lane clearly stamped 'L.&S.W.R.'
Timothy P. Cooper

working at this crossing as the German bombers regularly visited the nearby shipyards on the River Medina to drop their lethal loads. Oh yes, we certainly knew there was a war on when the anti-aircraft guns opened up and bits of shrapnel started to rain down on the railway line.

When Miss Dew gave up the crossing keeper's job, I was asked to take over, but I declined as this involved being residential and getting up in the night to let the early morning mail train through. Nevertheless, I continued to work one of the two shifts covered at the crossing, either 6am until 2pm or, 2pm until 10pm. In addition to this I earnt some extra money working at Newport, cleaning the carriage stock. When the Cowes line closed in 1966, I transferred to Ryde Pier Head and continued to work there until retirement.

One thing worthy of mention, although nothing to do with the crossing, was the Gasworks Siding adjacent to the crossing. It was worked by a ground frame released off an Annett's key, and there was coal traffic 'tripped' as required by the Medina Wharf engine. To save line occupation and bearing in mind the modest distance involved, this siding wasn't always worked with the Cowes goods train.

No. 29 *Alverstone* passes over Smithards Lane Crossing with a Newport and Ryde bound train in October 1965.

Timothy P. Cooper

No. 26 *Whitwell* departs from Mill Hill with the 10.30am to Cowes train on 31st August 1965.

John Goss

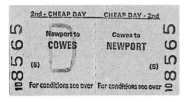

It was a case of operating convenience in practice, regardless of whatever the official Working Timetable may have said. I have perfectly vivid memories of the Wharf shunting engine propelling one wagon of coal from Medina Wharf Junction up to the siding and back within four or five minutes. The guard would travel on the footplate of the locomotive and with no brake van (quite illegal), the operation could be carried out easily and speedily! This type of practice was typical Isle of Wight railway procedure, but it worked.

The memories of a whistle from an approaching train, a wave from the footplate crew and guard will never die. Although my job was but a small part in the running of the Island railway, I felt a full member of the team.

Larry Watson

Cowes station was perhaps the prettiest station on the Island and I had the privilege of working there for 24 years as a signalman. We had three men working the shifts in the box from just before 4.30am until 10.30pm. There were two full signalmen, Larry Woodley and myself, and a porter-signalman. Prior to working at Cowes I worked for short periods, first at Ryde Works and then as a

MILL HILL

One of the busy commuter stations of the Island. Passengers would leave for their place of employment, and incoming trains would disgorge hundreds of humans employed in the shipbuilding yards which made Cowes the main source of employment on the Island.

No. 27 *Merstone* bursts out into the open from the smoke-filled gloom of the 208-yard long Mill Hill Tunnel, hauling the 9.24am from Cowes on 29th August 1965.

John Goss

No. 22 *Brading* heads down the 1:108 gradient into Cowes on 20th February 1966. This photograph was taken at the Cowes end of Mill Hill Tunnel which was comparatively rarely photographed.

John Goss

No. 22 *Brading* heads up the gradient out of Cowes bound for Newport and Ryde on 20th February 1966.

John Goss

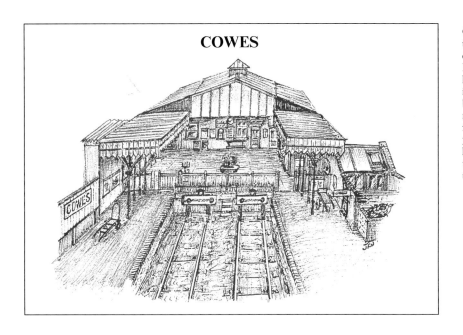

COWES

Officially opened in 1862 the Cowes to Newport line was the first stretch of track to be inaugurated in the Island. As the town grew in popularity as a yachting centre, to reach its peak when the Royal Family became yachting enthusiasts, the railway station had always to cater for many thousands of visitors every year. After the Second World War however, and the increasing use of the private motor car, the end was unfortunately inevitable.

No. 14 *Fishbourne* simmers in the platform at Cowes station after arrival with a train from Ryde in March 1965. Signalman Larry Woodley, or Signalman Bert Watson, has just pulled the ground signal 'off' so that No. 14 can push the stock backwards clear of the cross-over points.
John Goss

junior porter at Whitwell on the Ventnor West branch, but working at Cowes was far more intensive working.

The area around Cowes was a hive of industry during the Second World War as the yacht building yards and slipways were converted to Royal Naval use. This therefore made the area a prime target for German bombing raids, and consequently the Island railway suffered periodically from stray bombs. After one such bombing raid on 5th May 1942, I discovered an unexploded 1,000 lb delayed-action bomb alongside the railway line between Smithard's Lane crossing and Medina Wharf. The line was re-opened for traffic between Newport and Cowes at 6.50am, and I was called upon to act as pilotman over the section of line. I remember setting off from Newport with the first train over the line since the raid and being told to proceed with caution past the unexploded bomb, but it was safe for railway traffic. However, as we approached the ten-foot deep crater the O2 tank engine went over three warning detonators placed upon the line. We were then given revised instructions and told to set back to Newport. As per the War Incident File records in the Appendix of *Once Upon A Line... Volume Two* pages 138 and 139, the train service was restored with the 1.08pm ex-Newport on 6th May 1942, but I had to continue as pilotman as the single-line signalling tablet apparatus took longer to restore.

It was also during the War that Mill Hill Tunnel was found to be in danger of collapse and emergency repairs had to be made. Special semi-circular strengthening segments were manufactured at Ryde Works and placed underneath the track inside the tunnel. This work involved temporary closure of the line and much night work before and after the placement of the concrete segments.

During the War many ladies were called up to work on the Island railways and some worked as guards. The usual procedure at Cowes station was for trains to enter the station on number 1 platform, and the locomotive would run round the train, while the empty carriage stock ran down the gradient towards the station buffer stop. During wartime the early morning services were quite intense with incoming workers for the shipyards and consequently both platforms 1 and 2 were in regular use. I remember a train with a lady guard aboard entering the station on platform 2. She followed the same procedure of operation as she was used to for platform 1, but did not take into account that the line curvature and gradient were more severe. The empty carriage stock therefore began to run down the gradient into the station

much faster towards the stop blocks. Seeing what was about to happen I jumped into the guard's compartment just in time to pull the Westinghouse brake on. However the carriages still managed to hit those stop blocks at a fair old speed, but if I hadn't reacted when I did then the carriages would have ended up out in the road outside the station!

The highlight of railway operation at Cowes each year was for the Cowes Fireworks, on the Friday night of the final day of the Cowes Week Sailing Regatta. Each year the railway had the headache of getting thousands of people to Cowes and back from all parts of the Island. The regular pattern of railway operation was suspended from 5pm, when the Newport–Cowes single-line section was given special authority by the railway authorities at Wimbledon, to have a train on the single-line section but shunting could take place within the station confines. I had to go through all the 'red tape' procedure of signing this special authorisation under, 'Electric Tablet Regulation Number Five – Section Clear But Junction Blocked'. In addition to this a hand signal was given at the outer home signal when the signal was on. While the firework display was on the signal box at Cowes was a good vantage point from which to watch. Before the War, when all the Island railways were open to traffic, five trains were assembled at Cowes ready to return passengers to all parts of the Island following the conclusion of the fireworks display. These trains would be dispatched from Cowes every eleven minutes or as soon as the single line to Newport was clear. As I remember, there were two trains for Ventnor, a train for Shanklin, one for Ryde and one to Newport, which returned later for the final passenger loadings. Connecting trains were provided in those days at Newport for Freshwater and Ventnor West, but after the War things were not quite the same.

From 1956 onwards, following the closure of the Newport–Sandown line, all the special trains had to run through to Ryde where Shanklin and Ventnor trains had to double back on themselves at St John's Road. Nevertheless, right up to the closure of Cowes station the Cowes Fireworks special workings were hectic and demanding for all the railway staff. The big headache for the steam engine crews was to conserve water in the tanks, but keep up a sufficient head of steam to haul those heavy six-coach trains up the gradient out of Cowes. The sparks from the exhaust of those little engines roaring up the gradient towards Mill Hill was always a guaranteed firework display in their own right! I wonder if nowadays the buses can cope as well with this mass exodus from Cowes.

Driver Ted Dale looks out of the cab of No. 27 *Merstone* as he rounds the sharply curved line into Cowes station on 20th February 1966. The loaded coal wagon behind the locomotive stands in the 32ft-long siding serving T. Gange & Sons, the local coal merchants.

John Goss

Opposite page, top: No. 27 *Merstone* pushes the empty carriage stock clear of the cross-over points at Cowes.

John Goss

Right: Having backed over the cross-over points Driver Dale opens No. 27's regulator as she runs around the empty carriage stock.

John Goss

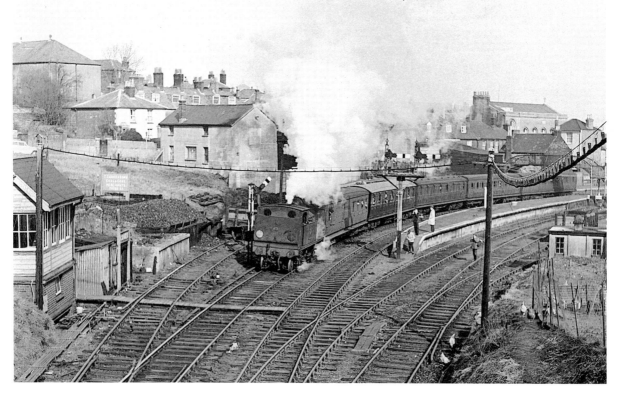

Left, top: After running round the three-coach set, *Merstone* detaches the Chatham brake coach and draws forward before descending into the sidings to collect two spare LBSCR composite carriages. The train is now reformed to a strengthened five-coach set for the return working to Ryde.
John Goss

Left, below: No. 27 *Merstone's* safety valves are lifted to indicate that she has a good head of steam. Driver Ted Dale pulls the whistle cord energetically to mark his final departure from Cowes station on the last day of operation of the Newport and Cowes service. Guard Sam Wells can also be seen looking back along the train from the front carriage guard's compartment. No doubt he was also saying his last fond farewell to Cowes.

John Goss

Full regulator up the gradient out of Cowes, as No. 27 *Merstone* heads towards Mill Hill and Newport, under the control of Driver Ted Dale.

John Goss

Chapter Six – The Freshwater Branch (Newport–Yarmouth–Freshwater)

Fred Gander

My origins date back to the London, Brighton & South Coast Railway and I was based in the Publicity Department. After the Southern took over I moved to Portsmouth in charge of station publicity and it was this that took me over to the Isle of Wight. My job was to place the old enamel advertising signs at strategic points on stations and railway property. This briefly brought me into contact with station staff and operating staff at close quarters. I even had contact with the Carriage & Wagon Department in the Works and instructed them on which adverts were to be placed in the various carriage compartments – at least eight per train. At one time we tried an experiment on the carriage door mass advertising theme for Lipton's tea. It didn't really go somehow on the Isle of Wight and was withdrawn.

After the Second World War I came over to the Island at least twice a week to look after each railway station's advertising requirements. I would usually catch a service train and travel with the guard in the brake van with a collection of enamel posters for a given station. With the help of station porters I would then set to work in mounting and securing them. In later years the job got easier with paper posters just being distributed to the various stations. I used to like our own posters in latter days – Cuneo railway scenes and David Shepherd locomotive prints. Local advertisers and hotels continued to advertise on the railway right up to the end of 1965/early 1966. Even up to the end of line service and closure there was no vandalism of posters. One could leave a poster up from one year to the next quite safely.

The strangest job I was ever given to do on the Island railways was to fix up Aspro advertisements in every Island railway ladies' toilet. They were in glass frames and were to be positioned at eye level when the lady was seated. It was a bit of a job to obtain access into the ladies' toilets. Ryde Esplanade station was the worst place, as in those days there were eleven separate ladies' toilets. In hind sight I guess I should have brought across a 'Gents' sign and placed it outside while I was at work.

I finished at the end of steam traction in 1967 and ended up by collecting the redundant enamel signs from the various stations. The wooden based posters were burned, but the enamel advertisements I either gave away or dumped off Ryde Pier Head station into the sea! If only I had known how valuable they would become.

The two things that I will always remember about the Island railways are the friendly staff and the time when I fell off Ryde Pier into the sea when attaching an enamel sign to the side railings!

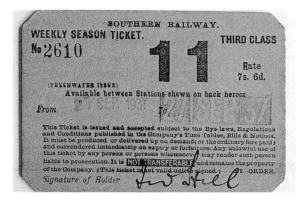

NEWPORT (FYNR)

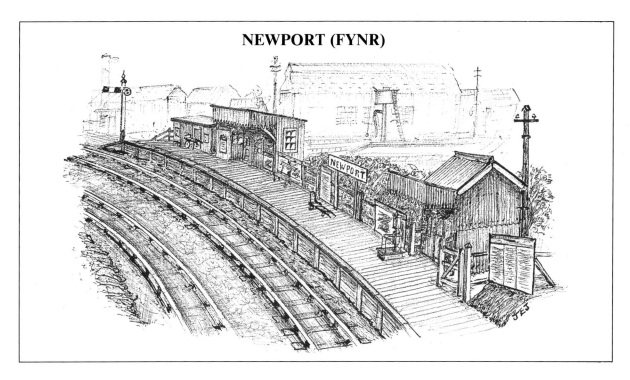

In the year 1913 the Freshwater, Yarmouth & Newport Railway built this timber platformed station at the Newport end of its line because the then Isle of Wight Central Railway refused to allow them to run over their tracks and into the main station. This situation was later resolved through amalgamation and when the Southern took control the whole station was demolished. The IWC engine shed and workshops are in the background.

Although quite close to Carisbrooke Castle, it is hard to realise that this small station once boasted a staff which included a fully fledged gold-braided Station Master.

CARISBROOKE

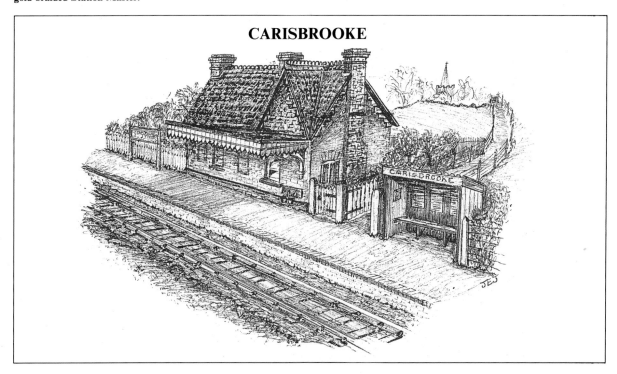

CARISBROOKE

As it appeared around 1910.

No. 27 *Merstone* again, surrounded by typical Island scenery. A sight once seen, never forgotten.

J. R. G. Griffiths

WATCHINGWELL

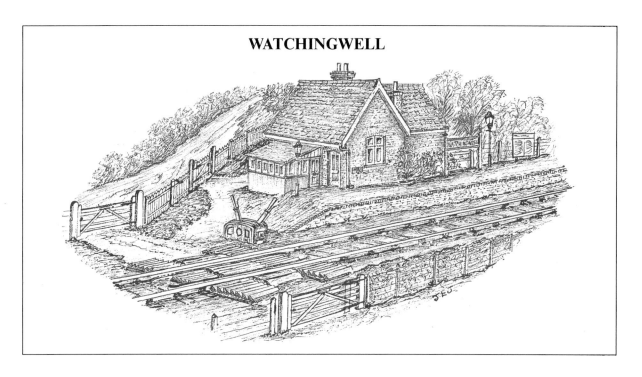

A small private station on the way to Freshwater. There was one thing it could boast about however, and that was the fact that cattle grids were fitted to its crossing around 1935, whilst they were not fitted to any other Island crossing until the electrification programme of 1965.

Watchingwell station was built for the private use of the Swainstone Estate and had a platform length of 95ft together with a 140ft siding.

J. R. G. Griffiths

CALBOURNE

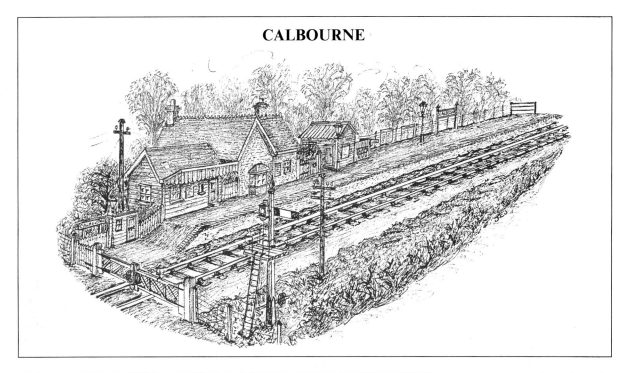

This station was sited quite a distance from any dwellings, but one gets the impression that it served several villages situated on either side of it.

Ningwood station in the mid-1930s, looking towards Freshwater. The Southern Railway extended the passing loop to accommodate longer trains and also installed a water tank at the Newport end of the 'up' platform.

J. R. G. Griffiths

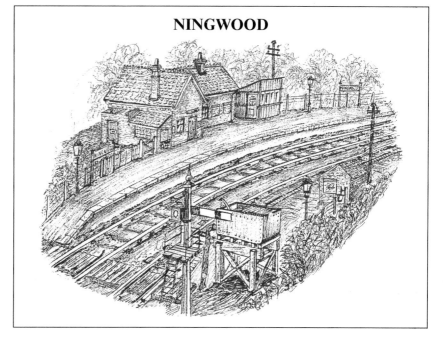

NINGWOOD

A busy scene at Ningwood station with a four-coach train for Newport, hauled by a 'Terrier' tank about to leave, and a Freshwater bound train seen departing around the curve.

J. R. G. Griffiths

A typical rural station, probably patronized a lot before bus routes were organised, but in latter years it was kept as the only crossing station on the Newport–Freshwater line.

A general view of Ningwood station.

J. R. G. Griffiths

About to depart from Ningwood, on the left, is the RCTS special of May 1952, hauled by No. 32 *Bonchurch*. The rear coach is the LBSCR bogie saloon carriage. On the right No. 30 *Shorwell*, driven by Monty Harvie, has just pulled to a halt with a service train to Freshwater. The guard alighting from the train is Bill Symes.

J. R. G. Griffiths

A collection of redundant rolling stock was taken out to Ningwood station siding in the early 1950s and 'dumped'. Ex-LBSCR four-wheel horse box No. 3370 stands stored out of service.

J. R. G. Griffiths

This delightful four-wheel horsebox was transferred to the Isle of Wight in 1925 and saw occasional use on Ashey Race Days.

J. R. G. Griffiths

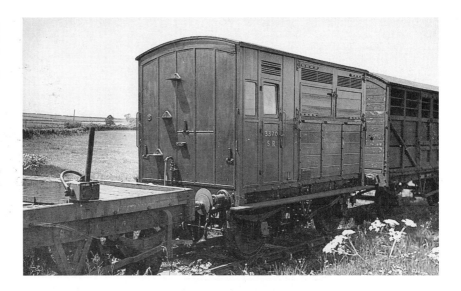

A side view of No. 3370 which saw little use after World War II and was eventually withdrawn from service in 1955.

J. R. G. Griffiths

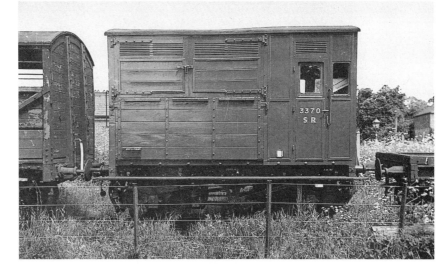

Also in store at Ningwood station siding were two ex-LBSCR 10-ton cattle wagons which were condemned in 1956.

J. R. G. Griffiths

The line of stored wagons at Ningwood also included two former Isle of Wight Central Railway water carrier wagons, which were eventually reinstated for use on a weed killing train. Note the axle box has 'I.W.R.' stamped on it.

J. R. G. Griffiths

Although the station was on the outskirts of the town, it was important for the fact that passengers travelling to the mainland had to alight there and make their way across the town to the ferry terminal.

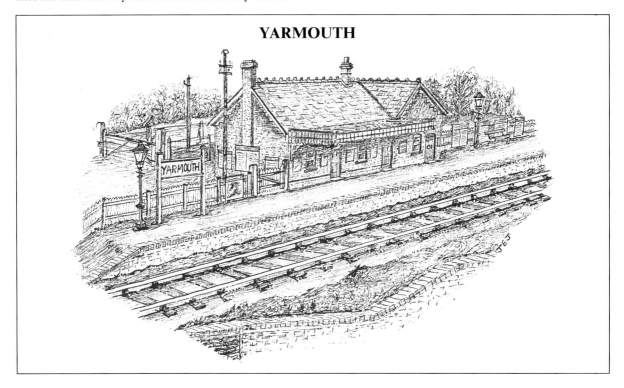

YARMOUTH

No. 31 *Chale* seen leaving Yarmouth with the 11.17am Newport–Freshwater train on 7th September 1953. The fireman looking out of the cab is David 'Dusty' Miller and the guard is H. Woodley.

Peter Joyce Collection

The dummy signal is pulled off for Driver Arthur Turner to gently ease No. 32 *Bonchurch* over the points to run round the LCGB special of May 1952, at Freshwater station.

J. R. G. Griffiths

FRESHWATER

Terminus of the Freshwater–Newport line and very well patronized during the summer months with visitors wishing to see the famous coloured sands of Totland and Allum Bays. The 'Tourist Train', which ran almost nonstop from Ventnor every day, was a very popular innovation, and its arrival almost became an event. The platform had eventually to be lengthened to accommodate it.

The exterior of Freshwater station on Sunday, 18th May 1952. Guard George Pocock is seen on the far left, wandering down to the local shops.

J. R. G. Griffiths

Appendix One

BRITISH TRANSPORT COMMISSION.
BRITISH RAILWAYS: SOUTHERN REGION.

Office of Assistant for Isle of Wight.
NEWPORT. I.W.

TO ALL MEMBERS OF THE STAFF OF
ALL DEPARTMENTS IN THE I.O.W.

21st September, 1959.

SUMMER TRAFFIC – ISLE OF WIGHT.

As we have now come to the end of a most successful Summer, I felt that some details regarding our traffic would be of interest, and, therefore, set out various details below for the information of all staff.

I think it can be agreed that the past Summer has been one of the best in living memory, certainly the finest since 1921, that wonderful Summer that gave us the visit of the Australian Tourists, including J. M. Gregory and E. A. McDonald, and no doubt some of you will remember the havoc they caused on the iron pitches of that time.

After a somewhat slow start, in May, traffic quickly picked up, and we in the Island have, I feel, cause for satisfaction concerning the general picture, as the Railway more than played its part, at times under great difficulty, in assisting the holiday efforts of the Island as a whole, details of our main Summer figures being as follows:-

PORTSMOUTH – RYDE ROUTE.	PASSENGERS.		
	TO RYDE	FROM RYDE	TOTAL
SAT. May 30	12,974	8,866	21,840
June 6	17,002	11,445	28,447
13	20,314	16,571	36,885
20	23,539	17,776	41,315
27	23,315	21,163	44,478
July 4	23,908	18,777	42,685
11	22,760	20,253	43,013
18	27,234	21,900	49,134
25	37,178	25,582	62,760
Aug. 1	26,541	25,516	52,057
8	32,340	32,903	65,243
15	27,758	26,458	54,216
22	26,445	28,471	54,916
29	24,337	29,365	53,702
Sept. 5	19,229	27,539	46,768
12	13,318	19,815	33,133

The above set out somewhat differently gives us figures as shewn hereunder which is certainly a most pleasing result, bearing in mind the rather slow start already mentioned:-

	1958	1959
PORTSMOUTH – RYDE. 16 Sats. (30. May–12. Sept)	368,009	378,192
RYDE – PORTSMOUTH.	343,779	352,400
	711,878	730,592

This shows an increase of 18,714 over last year, to a total of 730,592 passengers, the increase being split up into 10,093 to the Island, and 8,621 away.

Our weekday tripper traffic has also been very heavy indeed, the figures for the journey Portsmouth, Ryde and Return, (Mondays–Fridays), for the months May to August being 1,237,213, which shows an increase of 174,113 over last year's similar period, the figures month by month being as under:-

DAY TRIPPER TRAFFICE (MONDAYS – FRIDAYS).
PORTSMOUTH, RYDE & RETURN.

1958.					1959.			
MAY	JUNE	JULY	AUGUST		MAY	JUNE	JULY	AUGUST
166,705	188,607	312,767	395,021		185,782	223,232	356,448	471,751

Traffic on the ferry routes has also been extremely heavy, and to give some idea of the increase on, say, the two peak Saturdays of July 25th and August 8th, the figures this year over 1957, (corresponding days), for the two routes (Portsmouth/Fishbourne – Lymington/Yarmouth and vice versa), show increases of 2,103 passengers, 343 motorcycles and 67 cars, and this rise has shown itself throughout the Summer to varying degrees from time to time.

Day tripper and holiday traffic has been mixed on Sundays, but here again traffic has been very heavy, the highest total reached on any one Sunday being 28,605 against the previous year's 27,072. (Portsmouth – Ryde route).

It only remains for me to add my own thanks to all staff for the excellent way in which many difficult jobs have been overcome, long hours at times having to be worked, and I assure each and every one of you that the efforts made are much appreciated by Headquarters both at District and Waterloo level.

Assistant for Isle of Wight.

Appendix Two

BRITISH RAILWAYS – SOUTHERN REGION.

Office of Assistant for Isle of Wight.
NEWPORT. I.W.

TO ALL MEMBERS OF THE STAFF OF
ALL DEPARTMENTS IN THE ISLE OF WIGHT.

28th August, 1960.

PEAK SUMMER TRAFFIC – ISLE OF WIGHT.

Weekend traffic this year, so far as holidaymakers are concerned, has been well up to average, which is most satisfactory, but owing to the very bad weather conditions, day tripper traffic has, of course, been well down, the Summer being an unfortunate one in this respect from our point of view.

As on previous occasions I set out below details of our passenger carryings on the Portsmouth–Ryde route for Summer Saturdays June 25th to date, these being as follows.

	PASSENGERS		
DATE	PORTSMOUTH–RYDE	RYDE–PORTSMOUTH	TOTAL
SAT. JUNE 25th	23,150	20,658	43,808
JULY 2nd	24,359	20,729	45,088
9th	23,389	20,060	43,449
16th	28,205	21,706	49,911
23rd	36,417	25,586	62,003
30th	26,271	23,223	49,494
AUG. 6th	30,860	31,629	62,489
13th	26,663	24,276	50,939
20th	26,813	27,119	53,932

As most of you will be aware, the highest carryings on this route for an individual Saturday occurred on 11th August, 1956, 67,645 passengers passing between Portsmouth and Ryde and vice versa, this total being made up of 32,385 (from Portsmouth) and 35,260 (to Portsmouth), but this total has been reduced in recent years mainly due to the fact that more holidaymakers are now travelling to and from the Island on the previous Friday, for obvious reasons, which has, of course, made for an easier working so far as we are concerned.

This year the highest number carried on one day was 62,489 on Saturday, 6th August, 30,860 (from Portsmouth) and 31,629 (to Portsmouth), and to show the increases that have taken place in our Friday traffic, as mentioned earlier, figures covering the Friday previous to the peak Saturday for years 1956/60 inclusive are set out below, as a matter of interest.

Cont.

	FROM PORTSMOUTH	TO PORTSMOUTH	TOTAL
1956	5,945	11,151	17,096
1957	6,378	12,537	18,915
1958	7,101	12,540	19,641
1959	10,444	14,824	25,268
1960	10,828	15,073	25,901

As is already known, our train timekeeping has left something to be desired during the past month or so, the importance of right time working is, therefore, again stressed, and all staff are asked to do everything possible to ensure such applying for the remainder of the season, as although the peak is now past, considerable traffic should be forthcoming within the next month or so, and with the hope of an improvement in the weather, a fairly good late season may be expected, as from information received from certain Hotels in the East Wight, bookings are still heavy until well into next month.

Assistant for Isle of Wight.

160